The
5-Minute
Prayer
Plan
for
When Life Is
Overwhelming

Published by Barbour Publishing, Inc., 1810 Barbour Drive, Uhrichsville, Ohio 44683, www.barbourbooks.com

Our mission is to inspire the world with the life-changing message of the Bible.

 Member of the
Evangelical Christian
Publishers Association

Printed in the United States of America.

A Guide to More Focused Prayer

The
5-Minute
Prayer
Plan
for
When Life Is
Overwhelming

Linda Lyle

BARBOUR
PUBLISHING

Introduction

Prayer is meant to be a dynamic exchange between the majestic Creator and His creation. No doubt you've experienced those moments of divine connection at different seasons in your life. Yet, you still at times fall into a repetitious routine where you just want your time in prayer to be more but aren't sure how to get there.

This practical and inspirational book will open up new ways into prayer with ninety "5-Minute" plans for your daily quiet time. You'll explore prayer plans focused on varied aspects of life. A handy subject index in the back of the book will help you find these topics quickly.

Each entry includes:

- Minute 1: A scripture to meditate on

- Minute 2–3: Specific prayer points and questions to consider as you enter a time of prayer

- Minute 4–5: A jump-starter prayer to springboard you into a time of conversation with God

The prayers in this book have been written with you in mind, each word penned in prayer, asking the Lord to give insight into the needs of those who will begin a new or renewed journey with Him. Deep, heartfelt prayer happens in those quiet moments when you stand transparently before the one with arms wide open to embrace you in unconditional love.

Watering the Wasteland

*Remember ye not the former things, neither consider
the things of old. Behold, I will do a new thing; now
it shall spring forth; shall ye not know it? I will even
make a way in the wilderness, and rivers in the desert.*

ISAIAH 43:18–19

- While it's good to remember the past, we aren't meant to dwell on it. We can remember the wonderful times with joy and identify the lessons we can learn from the storms and disappointments of life. But we should not dwell on either to the point that we lose sight of the present. Is there anything you need to release from your past so that you can live fully in the moment?

- God is always going before us to do something new in our lives. Just as He was a cloud by day and a pillar of fire by night for the Israelites in the wilderness, God moves before us. He knows what is coming and is making a path for our future, but we must keep moving forward. What is the next step God is leading you to take?

- We must be intentional in looking for the movement of God. He wants to show us where He is at work and invites us to join Him. Take a moment to look at your life and identify areas where you feel God's hand at work. What do you see God doing in your life right now? Your church? Your community?

- God can renew parts of our lives that we feel are like a wasteland. Often, aspects of our spiritual lives can become dry and barren, but Jesus is the living water. He can bring those things back to life. Sometimes parts of our past can seem a waste, but God can work all things to our good if we will give it to Him. What parts of your life need the waters of renewal?

Father, help me to learn from the past but keep moving forward. Show me the next step to take, and give me the strength and courage to make a leap of faith knowing that You have already gone ahead of me. You are making a way for me through the desert. You are renewing parts of my life I thought were a wasteland. Help me to see Your movement in my life and to follow Your lead.

Living in the Encampment of the Lord

I sought the Lord, and he heard me, and delivered me from all my fears. They looked unto him, and were lightened: and their faces were not ashamed. This poor man cried, and the Lord heard him, and saved him out of all his troubles. The angel of the Lord encampeth round about them that fear him, and delivereth them. O taste and see that the Lord is good: blessed is the man that trusteth in him.

PSALM 34:4–8

- David was often under attack from enemies, as many of the psalms attest to, but he made it a habit to take his troubles to the Lord. If we seek the Lord, He will hear us and deliver us. We see this in the scripture, but we can also see it in our own lives. When have you called on the Lord and He delivered you? What are your fears and worries today? Seek the Lord and tell Him your situation. He is waiting to hear from you.

- As Christians and children of God, we are surrounded by the angels who protect us. We are also inhabited by the Holy Spirit, who comforts us and gives us guidance. We are not alone. God keeps and delivers us. How does this truth make you feel?

- God feeds us through His holy Word, and when we taste it, we are satisfied. There is nothing else on earth that can fill us. How can you feed on these verses today?

- God saves us, keep us, and satisfies us. Given these blessings, what has God done for you today that deserves your praise?

- We often say we trust God, but trust requires action on our part. It may mean letting go of something, like a burden or even a desire. When we give our burdens to the Lord, it frees us and lightens our load. When we give our dreams and talents to the Lord, He can use them for His glory. What do you need to trust God with today?

Father, You are gracious and kind. I know that You are good because I have seen the evidence in my life. You are the God who saves us, who keeps us, and who satisfies us. I have so much to be thankful for, yet I know You still listen to my cries. When I am in trouble, You invite me to seek You and You will hear me. As I lay my burdens before You, I know You will hear my prayers and You will answer me. It may not be the answer I desire, but You always have my best interest at heart, so I can trust You with what is on my heart today.

Sharing the Load

*And having an high priest over the house of God; let us
draw near with a true heart in full assurance of faith,
having our hearts sprinkled from an evil conscience,
and our bodies washed with pure water. Let us hold
fast the profession of our faith without wavering; (for
he is faithful that promised;) and let us consider one
another to provoke unto love and to good works: not
forsaking the assembling of ourselves together, as the
manner of some is; but exhorting one another: and
so much the more, as ye see the day approaching.*

HEBREWS 10:21–25

- In Jesus Christ we have a high priest we can
  approach without having to make an appointment
  or cut through red tape. We can draw near to Him
  and be washed clean. He doesn't keep us at a
  distance, and He is ready and willing to forgive us
  if we only ask. How does that change the way you
  think about confession?

- Another benefit of the Christian life is we can grow
  in faith, work through doubts and questions, and
  still deepen our relationship with God. Is there
  anything that you are struggling with right now?
  Take it to Him. He is waiting to help you.

- As Christians we are also part of the fellowship of believers, where we can encourage one another. Are you a member of a local church or small group Bible study? How does sharing your burdens with others lighten your load?

- Besides encouragement, we can also worship together. Corporate worship is a way to gather strength from one another so that we can face the struggles of life together. Is there a battle you are trying to fight alone?

- Sometimes we feel overwhelmed because we try to take too much on ourselves. We were meant to be part of a community of faith and to share each other's burdens. We were also meant to rest in the strength of our high priest. Is there something you need help with? Are there others who are willing to share your burden if you would allow it?

Father, I'm thankful for a high priest I can go to at any time and receive forgiveness. I'm also thankful for the fellowship of other Christians who can share my burdens and offer encouragement. Help me to remember that I am not in this alone.

When We Don't Know What to Pray

Likewise the Spirit also helpeth our infirmities: for we know not what we should pray for as we ought: but the Spirit itself maketh intercession for us with groanings which cannot be uttered. And he that searcheth the hearts knoweth what is the mind of the Spirit, because he maketh intercession for the saints according to the will of God. And we know that all things work together for good to them that love God, to them who are the called according to his purpose.

ROMANS 8:26–28

- The Holy Spirit is referred to as a helper. He helps us with many things, but isn't it wonderful to know that He intercedes on our behalf? He knows all our weaknesses and all our needs even when we can't voice them ourselves. Have you ever been so overwhelmed that you didn't even know what to pray? It's all right to feel that way, because you're not alone. All of us feel that way at some point, but the good news is we have someone who can pray for us.

- The Holy Spirit is also uniquely gifted to be an intercessor because He knows the will of God just as well as He knows us. Have you ever considered the freedom of being known and loved by someone with the power and knowledge to ask for exactly what we need when we need it?

- When we are in difficult seasons, it's hard to see the good, but God can use anything for our good. It may not be apparent right now because God is more concerned with the eternal than the temporal. Yet, He knows us and loves us, so we can be assured He will work it out for our best. Can you remember times God brought good out of difficult situations in your past? How can you trust Him with your current situation?

- The statement that God works all things together for good has a caveat. It applies to believers who are trying to walk in God's will for their lives. Are you looking for God's will in your situation?

Father, I don't always understand the circumstances in my life, but I know that You have my best interest at heart. Even when I don't know how to pray, You sent the Holy Spirit to intercede for me. Help me leave my circumstances in Your capable hands, knowing You will work everything for my good when I walk in Your will.

The Finisher

And David said to Solomon his son, Be strong and of
good courage, and do it: fear not, nor be dismayed: for
the Lord God, even my God, will be with thee; he will
not fail thee, nor forsake thee, until thou hast finished
all the work for the service of the house of the Lord.

1 CHRONICLES 28:20

- David was leaving Solomon with the huge task of building the temple. Solomon must have felt overwhelmed by the enormity of such an undertaking. David tells him not to be afraid or dismayed because God would be with him. Is there a task on your plate that seems too big to handle? Don't be afraid because if God has called you to it, then He will be with you.

- David also told him to "do it." Fear can be immobilizing, freezing us in our tracks. One of the keys to overcoming anxiety is to take action. If you sit and think too long, you can imagine all the worst-case scenarios that will probably never come to pass. If you take action, it will free you because it's harder to fear when you're busy at a task. Don't worry about the whole project. What is something that you can do today to move forward? Do that.

- David also pointed out that God would not fail or forsake Solomon. He would be with him until he finished what he was tasked to do. God will finish what He starts. How does that change your perception of the task, knowing God will be there to the finish line?

- What seems like a big task right now might be getting out of bed or just doing the day-to-day tasks, but God cares about those things as much as He did the building of the temple. What do you need to do today? Ask God to show you and to give you the strength to accomplish it.

Father, the task before me seems enormous, but I know You have called me to it. Help me see the one thing I need to focus on today. Give me the strength to do it. I trust You to be with me to the finish line because I know You finish what You start. Help me to take the first step in faith, knowing You will take every step with me.

A Light in the Darkness

Therefore I will look unto the Lord; I will wait for the God of my salvation: my God will hear me. Rejoice not against me, O mine enemy: when I fall, I shall arise; when I sit in darkness, the Lord shall be a light unto me. I will bear the indignation of the Lord, because I have sinned against him, until he plead my cause, and execute judgment for me: he will bring me forth to the light, and I shall behold his righteousness.

MICAH 7:7–9

- When we find ourselves in a dark place, the first thing we should do is look to the Lord. How often do you find yourself looking for help everywhere else first? Do you call your friends? Do you use a search engine to look for solutions? Do you rack your brain and stress yourself out? God should be our first stop when we face a battle, not our last hope.

- The next step is to wait on God. We live in a culture that is diametrically opposed to waiting. We want everything fast and easy, no waiting. God is not in a hurry, because He is always right on time. Have you ever rushed to handle a situation, only to make it worse? If we take a deep breath and wait on God, we will find the best answer even if it's not easy.

- Micah believed God would hear him, but he also believed God would be right beside him even through tough times. He knew tough times were inevitable, but he believed God would sit with him in the darkness. Do you believe God sits beside you in the darkness?

- Micah also believed that God would bring him out of the darkness and into the light. In this world, seasons come and go. There are seasons of difficulty and darkness, and there are seasons of joy and light. What season are you in? God is there with you.

- The enemy is always on the attack, but God fights for us. He will execute judgment in His way and in His time. Do you feel under attack? Remember that God is fighting for you.

Father, sometimes the way seems so dark, but I'm grateful for Your presence that brings light into the darkness. Thank You for fighting for me. I look to You for help and will wait on You to guide the way.

Planted

Blessed is the man that walketh not in the counsel of the ungodly, nor standeth in the way of sinners, nor sitteth in the seat of the scornful. But his delight is in the law of the LORD; and in his law doth he meditate day and night. And he shall be like a tree planted by the rivers of water, that bringeth forth his fruit in his season; his leaf also shall not wither; and whatsoever he doeth shall prosper.

PSALM 1:1–3

- Where we spend our time makes a difference in how we live our lives. The psalmist starts by pointing out where not to walk, stand, or sit. These verbs are not about short-term incidents; they are about our habits. Do you spend a lot of time with people who give ungodly advice or live in blatant sin? While we are called to witness to people who don't know God, we must be careful not to let their habits become ours.

- The psalmist then moves on to how we should spend a major portion of our time. Our delight should be in God's Word. We should spend time thinking about it and trying to live it out. How much time do you spend each day in the Bible? Why is it important?

- The psalmist concludes by pointing out the benefits of meditating on the scriptures: we will be well watered, fruitful, enduring, and prosperous. When we are rooted in the Word of God, we are firmly planted; and when storms come, we may be shaken, but we will not be uprooted. Then the fruits of the Spirit will be evident in our lives. We will be able to endure the seasons and continue to grow. Do you feel planted in the Word? Do storms make you feel uprooted? Studying and meditating on the scriptures will help you withstand even the strongest storms.

- When we are firmly planted in God's Word, we are unmovable when the storms come. Are you facing a storm right now? Dig into the Word and get grounded.

Father, I want to be like a tree planted by the waters. Help me to guard my heart and mind as I live in this world but am not of it. As I study Your Word, help me to take it deep into my roots so that it will help me remain unmovable when I face storms and battles.

My Shepherd

The LORD is my shepherd; I shall not want. He maketh me to lie down in green pastures: he leadeth me beside the still waters. He restoreth my soul: he leadeth me in the paths of righteousness for his name's sake. Yea, though I walk through the valley of the shadow of death, I will fear no evil: for thou art with me; thy rod and thy staff they comfort me. Thou preparest a table before me in the presence of mine enemies: thou anointest my head with oil; my cup runneth over. Surely goodness and mercy shall follow me all the days of my life: and I will dwell in the house of the LORD for ever.

PSALM 23

- This psalm is probably the most well-known and memorized psalm of all time. However, have you ever taken the time to really read and comprehend each verse?

- Have you ever contemplated the statement "The LORD is my shepherd"? He is not just a shepherd; He is your personal shepherd. You are not one of a huge number that He barely recognizes. You are a beloved sheep that He will seek and protect at all costs. When you feel surrounded by wolves, you have a shepherd who stands guard.

- Your shepherd also provides everything for you. That doesn't mean you will have everything you desire, but you will not want for what you need. He leads you to green pastures and still waters as a means of restoring your soul. Sometimes that place is physical and sometimes it's spiritual. When has your shepherd restored your soul?

- Your shepherd goes with you through the valley of the shadow of death. The emphasis is on the word *through* because the valley of shadow is not a place you live but a place you pass through. Your shepherd goes with you and brings His rod and staff to lead and protect you as you travel through difficult times. Are you walking through a valley of shadow? Keep walking, because this is only temporary.

Father, You are my shepherd, a personal leader who wants the best for me. You provide for my needs, which sometimes includes correction. Thank You for walking with me as well as watching over me. Even when I walk through dark valleys, You are with me. Restore my soul and keep me on the right path.

Broken Hearts and Contrite Spirits

The LORD is nigh unto them that are of a broken heart; and saveth such as be of a contrite spirit. Many are the afflictions of the righteous: but the LORD delivereth him out of them all.

PSALM 34:18–19

- When our hearts are broken by our sin, we feel ashamed and want to hide like Adam and Eve in the garden of Eden. The truth is that God is never closer than when we come before Him with a broken heart. It's not until we are convicted by our sin that we can be open and honest before God. Then we can be healed and move forward. Have you ever been brokenhearted about sin in your life?

- A contrite spirit is one that is humble and admits fault. Has someone ever come to you for forgiveness, but you could tell they were not so much sorry they had wronged you as they were sorry they had been caught? Did their apology ring true? Did you wonder if they would repeat their behavior in the future? Attitude does matter. When we go before God with a contrite spirit, we are saying we will change. Do you have a contrite spirit?

- This world is full of trouble, so afflictions will come our way even when we have a right spirit with God. However, God will deliver us from them. Sometimes He delivers us out of the situation, and sometimes He delivers through the situation. Has God delivered you out of trouble? Have you felt God's presence even as you walked through difficult times?

- Our first response to guilt is often excuses, but in the end, having a broken heart and a contrite spirit is always the better way to go. Is God speaking to your heart about something you know you need to change? Are you offering excuses or asking for forgiveness?

Father, we humans are proud beings, and we don't like to admit when we're wrong. Still, when we admit our failures, You are faithful and just to forgive us and heal us. I ask You to be at work in my heart and in my spirit that I might be more aware of Your gentle leading. Help me to keep a contrite spirit that is open to Your correction, so that when afflictions come, I know You will deliver me.

Unfailing Mercy

I will heal their backsliding, I will love them freely:
for mine anger is turned away from him. I will be
as the dew unto Israel: he shall grow as the lily, and
cast forth his roots as Lebanon. His branches shall
spread, and his beauty shall be as the olive tree, and his
smell as Lebanon. They that dwell under his shadow
shall return; they shall revive as the corn, and grow
as the vine: the scent thereof shall be as the wine of
Lebanon. Ephraim shall say, What have I to do any
more with idols? I have heard him, and observed him:
I am like a green fir tree. From me is thy fruit found.

HOSEA 14:4–8

- When we are weak, burdened, and over-whelmed, God still loves us. In these verses, He offers to heal us from our backsliding and love us freely. All we have to do is come to Him and He will renew our spirits. Is there something weighing on your spirit? Take it to God and let Him renew a right spirit within you. His mercies never fail.

- There are two ways we can err. The first is forgetting that God will not let us continue in our sin without consequences. The second is thinking that God is not big enough to handle our sin. God is ready and willing to forgive us when we ask. There is nothing that He can't handle. Which side do you fall on? Either way, God's mercies are unfailing.

- There are consequences both to ignoring God's Word and to following God's Word. If we continue in our sin, we will be in danger of His wrath. If we are obedient, we will flourish. Which way will you choose?

- When life is difficult, it's hard to maintain clarity and focus. It's easy to get discouraged and distracted by the things of the world. When we allow the world to overwhelm us, it's good to know that God's mercies are unfailing. What is troubling your mind? Bring it to God and let Him clear your mind and bring you peace even in difficult times.

Father, Your mercies are new every day. They are unfailing. No matter what we have done, You still wait to forgive us and heal us with Your love. You are justified in Your anger when we are disobedient, but You are faithful to forgive when we confess and return to You. Thank You for Your unfailing mercies.

Powered by Hope

But we have this treasure in earthen vessels, that the excellency of the power may be of God, and not of us. We are troubled on every side, yet not distressed; we are perplexed, but not in despair; persecuted, but not forsaken; cast down, but not destroyed.

2 CORINTHIANS 4:7–9

- Some people put treasure in a safe or in a fireproof box made of some kind of metal to keep out the elements. God put His treasure in an earthen vessel: us. He knew we were made from dust when He chose us. The treasure is the power of the Holy Spirit within us so that God may receive the glory, for it is Him working in us. Do you feel like you are not enough? Don't worry, because with God's power inside of you, you are more than enough.

- Do you ever feel like trouble surrounds you? We all feel that way sometimes, but the scripture tells us we don't have to be distressed. God is all around you, and you can trust Him with all your troubles. Do you have troubles that you need to turn over to God?

- Do you ever feel like you don't know what to do? The scripture tells us to not despair, because God is right there to guide us through the Holy Spirit within us. What is perplexing you today? Ask God for guidance.

- Do you feel persecuted? Many of us do not know what it's like to be in danger for our lives because of our beliefs. Still, we can feel persecuted for making decisions based on our faith rather than the world's values. It may be through not getting promoted, being ostracized, or even losing a job. Even when the world persecutes us, we are not forsaken. God has not forgotten us.

- Have you been struck down, whether physically, spiritually, or mentally? You may be down temporarily, but you are not destroyed. As long as we have God, our eternity is set in heaven. In the meantime, God will help you rise up again to continue His purpose for your life.

Father, thank You for choosing mere earthen vessels to be Your home. I know it is by Your strength that we are able to do anything. No matter what the world tries to do to us, we can rely on Your strength. Whether we are troubled, confused, persecuted, or attacked, I know You will carry us through in Your strength because I am powered by my hope in You.

Be Prepared

Humble yourselves therefore under the mighty hand of God, that he may exalt you in due time: casting all your care upon him; for he careth for you. Be sober, be vigilant; because your adversary the devil, as a roaring lion, walketh about, seeking whom he may devour: whom resist stedfast in the faith, knowing that the same afflictions are accomplished in your brethren that are in the world. But the God of all grace, who hath called us unto his eternal glory by Christ Jesus, after that ye have suffered a while, make you perfect, stablish, strengthen, settle you.

1 PETER 5:6–10

- When most people think of casting, they think of fishing, where you send your line and lure out over the water and then gradually wind it back to you. In this scripture there is another meaning to the word. Have you ever fed the ducks at the duck pond? What do you do? You cast the bread onto the water. Are you expecting to get the bread back? No. So why do we cast our cares on God and then try to take them back? What do you need to let go of today? Give it to God because He cares for you and will handle anything if we will let go.

- Have you ever been in a parking lot at night? Were you aware of your environment? Most of us would answer yes. We want to be alert to potential dangers so that we can avoid them. We should also be aware in our spiritual lives. The adversary is looking to devour us and make us useless to God's work. We have to resist his attacks through faith, but we can only do that if we recognize that he is the one at work. Have you been sober and vigilant?

- Even when you suffer afflictions, you can rest assured that God will perfect, establish, strengthen, and settle you. To perfect means to make complete, not to make without fault. God is working to make us complete through His power, and sometimes He uses affliction to accomplish it. Affliction also establishes us stronger and settles us firmly in the faith.

Father, I cast my cares on You. I give them to You with no desire to take them back. I know afflictions are bound to come my way, but I pray that You would help me be aware of the attacks of the adversary and to be prepared through Your Word and the Holy Spirit to resist him and hold on firmly to my faith.

Comforting the Multitude of Thoughts

Who will rise up for me against the evildoers? or who will stand up for me against the workers of iniquity? Unless the LORD had been my help, my soul had almost dwelt in silence. When I said, My foot slippeth; thy mercy, O LORD, held me up. In the multitude of my thoughts within me thy comforts delight my soul.

PSALM 94:16–19

- Do you find your mind filled with questions about circumstances or the future? Do you question injustice in the world? You are not alone; the psalmist was questioning who would stand up against injustice in his own life. His answer is that only the Lord can help us. Do you have questions about what is going on around you? Don't be afraid to ask God, because He loves you and wants to help you.

- Do you ever feel like no one hears you? The psalmist said that if not for God he would have lived in silence. Maybe you feel like no one sees your struggle or hears your cries for help, but God is always waiting to hear from you and is a patient listener. What is on your heart and mind today? Don't dwell in silence. Share it with God.

- Do you feel like you are slipping on the path? We all have days when we slip and fall, but God is there to pick us back up and put us back on the path. His mercy is ready to give us His hand of strength if we will only ask. What is tripping you up today?

- Do you find your mind swirling with worries? Sometimes our minds can be so preoccupied that we can't focus. When you have too many thoughts, take them to the Lord, maybe even write them down. He will comfort your soul and give you peace. What are you struggling with today? Make a list and give them to the Lord.

Father, my mind is full of thoughts, questions, and worries. There is so much anger and injustice in the world, but I know You are faithful and full of mercy. Calm my mind so that I can focus on You and Your purpose for my life. Help me to leave my questions and worries at Your feet. I need the comfort of Your presence.

Grace for Today

For this thing I besought the Lord thrice, that it might depart from me. And he said unto me, My grace is sufficient for thee: for my strength is made perfect in weakness. Most gladly therefore will I rather glory in my infirmities, that the power of Christ may rest upon me. Therefore I take pleasure in infirmities, in reproaches, in necessities, in persecutions, in distresses for Christ's sake: for when I am weak, then am I strong.

2 CORINTHIANS 12:8–10

- Paul had gone to the Lord three times and asked for the thorn in his flesh to be removed. Bible scholars are not sure exactly what ailed him, but God's answer was that His grace was sufficient. Is there something in your life that you have asked God to remove? Maybe a health issue or a relationship issue or even a work issue? Sometimes God doesn't remove the problem, but He does give us the power and strength to endure it through grace.

- Do you feel like you need to take care of things yourself, be self-sufficient? Sometimes the thorns in our flesh are to remind us of our need for God. Paul said he would rather glory in his infirmities so that he might have the power of God in his life.

- Paul took pleasure in infirmity, reproach, needs, and persecution because he knew that God's strength would be evident in his life. People would see God and not him. Are there circumstances in your life that fit any of these descriptions? Are you relying on your own strength, or have you given it over to God to handle?

- Grace isn't something that you can store up to use later. Grace is like the manna given in the wilderness; there is just enough for today. Every day there is a fresh supply of it available, but we must gather it in and apply it. What do you need grace for today?

Father, I thank You that Your grace is sufficient and that it is available at all times. Help me to remember that I can only do things in Your strength. Help me, like Paul, to take pleasure in weakness because I know You will be what people see. Most of all, help me to accept Your grace and release the need to be self-sufficient, for You are all I need.

The Other Side

*And the same day, when the even was come, he saith
unto them, Let us pass over unto the other side. And
when they had sent away the multitude, they took him
even as he was in the ship. And there were also with
him other little ships. And there arose a great storm of
wind, and the waves beat into the ship, so that it was
now full. And he was in the hinder part of the ship,
asleep on a pillow: and they awake him, and say unto
him, Master, carest thou not that we perish? And he
arose, and rebuked the wind, and said unto the sea,
Peace, be still. And the wind ceased, and there was
a great calm. And he said unto them, Why are ye so
fearful? how is it that ye have no faith? And they feared
exceedingly, and said one to another, What manner of
man is this, that even the wind and the sea obey him?*

MARK 4:35–41

- Jesus told the disciples to set sail to the other side
  of the lake. Jesus knew a storm was coming, yet
  He told them to set sail anyway. God can see the
  storms coming, but He still asks us to go forward,
  sometimes directly into the storm. What storm are
  you dealing with right now? Know that God was
  not surprised by it and that He has a purpose for it.

- The disciples were upset that Jesus was not upset.
  Do you ever get frustrated when it seems like God

34

isn't concerned about what you're going through? It seems as though He is asleep at the wheel. Jesus was both man and God. As a human, He needed rest, but as God, He was still in full control of the situation. The disciples were safe in His presence, but they were looking at the circumstances instead of the company. Where are you looking today? Are you looking at the storm, or are you looking at the one who controls the outcome?

- Part of the reason for the storm was to help the disciples build their faith and learn to trust. When we focus on God, the fears subside. Do you struggle with the question of trust? Keep your eyes on God, and you will soon find yourself safely on the other side of whatever challenge you face.

Father, help me keep my eyes on You and not the circumstances around me. You know all about the storm, and You will be with me to the other side.

Unmovable

Cast thy burden upon the LORD, and he shall sustain thee: he shall never suffer the righteous to be moved.

PSALM 55:22

- Do you ever feel like your burdens are crushing you? Did you know God wants to carry those for you? Throughout scripture God tells us to let Him carry our burdens. We weren't meant to carry heavy loads, but we also have to give them over. He can't carry what we won't release. What are you carrying today that you need to give over to God?

- Sometimes we carry burdens out of a sense of self-sufficiency. In our pride we want to do it ourselves, much like a two-year-old. When we remember that we can do nothing without God, then we can come to Him in humility. What are you struggling to do by yourself? Are you holding on in pride?

- Sometimes carrying burdens is a question of trust. Do you trust God to do what is best for you? Sometimes we hold on to things because we can't see what He is doing. Yet when we remember who He is, we know we can trust Him. However, we have to cast it away. We have to throw it into His hands and let go. Will you trust God and throw Him your burdens?

- Do you trust Him to sustain you? In what tangible ways can you trust Him?

- When we give everything to God and stand firm in our faith, He will not only sustain us but He will make us unmovable. No matter what is going on around us, we can be firm and unshaken if we trust Him. What is holding you back from letting go? Confess it to God and ask for help. He is ready and willing to give you His strength if only you ask for it.

Father, I struggle with pride and trust issues. Help me to cast my burdens on You and let go of them. I believe, but help my unbelief. Despite my desire for self-sufficiency, I cannot carry these burdens alone. I need Your strength. Help me to let go and stand unmovable in faith no matter what the circumstances.

Higher Ground

From the end of the earth will I cry unto thee, when
my heart is overwhelmed: lead me to the rock
that is higher than I. For thou hast been a shelter
for me, and a strong tower from the enemy.

PSALM 61:2–3

- The psalmist says from the end of the earth he cries. Do you feel like you have come to the end of the earth, the end of your rope? The good news is that where you come to the end of yourself is where you will find God. Sometimes we have to let go of *our* rope so that we can rest in the arms of the Savior. What are you holding on to?

- Is your heart overwhelmed? There are many days when doubts and fears and the to-do list all seem like too much. We want to curl up in a blanket and hope it goes away, but there is a much better option. We can go to the rock that is higher. Christ is the rock, and He is much higher than the world. We can go to Him, and He will lift us to higher ground in the shelter of His arms. He can handle whatever is going on in your life.

- Do you need shelter? Sometimes we just need a place to escape for a little while to get out of the storm. God is our shelter. David had to flee his home during his son Absalom's rebellion. He needed a physical shelter as well as a spiritual one. He needed a place to rest as well as a tower to protect him from his enemies. David knew where to go, and so do we. God is our rock, our shelter, and our tower.

Father, sometimes I feel like I am far from home and peace, but I know You hear me. My heart is overwhelmed just like David by the storms of life. Lead me to higher ground, to the rock that is higher than I. Lead me to Your feet, where shelter and refuge from the enemy are always available. Today I need Your strong arms to hold me and shield me.

Fear Not, for I Am

*Fear thou not; for I am with thee: be not
dismayed; for I am thy God: I will strengthen
thee; yea, I will help thee; yea, I will uphold thee
with the right hand of my righteousness.*

ISAIAH 41:10

- Are you ever afraid? The enemy uses fear to manipulate us, to freeze us in our steps, and to make us useless for the kingdom. The world is full of fear, but we are not of the world. We don't have to be afraid, for the I AM is with us always. What are you afraid of? Is it anything God can't handle? Of course not, so take your fears to Him and let Him handle what is beyond your abilities.

- Are you ever dismayed? Do you ever let circumstances ruin your day when things don't go the way you planned? God's plans are higher than our plans, and just because it isn't going your way doesn't mean it isn't going the way it should. The enemy also likes to use defeat and despair to make us ineffective in the kingdom and to steal our joy. Is the I AM your God? If He is, then there is no need to feel dismayed.

- Do you feel alone in your struggles? God is always with us. Even when others may betray us or fail us,

God can always be relied on. When we accept Christ as Lord, we have free access to the throne of God and all of its power any time of the day or night.

- Do you feel weak? When we are at our weakest, we can find true strength in Christ. As humans we run out of energy, but we have access to a power station with infinite energy. God wants to support us and help us, but we must remember it is His strength and not our own. All we have to do is ask.

Father, I'm human. I get tired, afraid, and full of despair, but You are the great I AM and the source of all energy and power. I need Your help. I know I don't have to fear or be dismayed, because You are always with me, but sometimes I forget. Remind me of Your presence and strengthen me by Your power. I will fear not, for You are the I AM.

Joy in the Morning

*Sing unto the Lord, O ye saints of his, and give thanks
at the remembrance of his holiness. For his anger
endureth but a moment; in his favour is life: weeping
may endure for a night, but joy cometh in the morning.*

PSALM 30:4–5

- For some reason, circumstances can just seem
  worse in the night hours. Sometimes those night
  hours are actually seasons of night when we cannot
  seem to find the light. The psalmist says to sing to
  the Lord and give thanks for what He has done for
  us in the past. Sing and give thanks? That's a tall
  order when we're struggling, but when we recall
  what He has done in the past, it reminds us that
  He can do it in our current struggles. What do you
  recall about God's work in your life?

- Do you feel like God is angry at you? While God is
  angry at sin in our lives, He loves us. He knows what
  sin is doing to us and our relationship with Him.
  However, His anger is short-lived. We need only ask
  for forgiveness. When we're in right relationship
  with Him, there is life. Is there some unconfessed
  sin in your life that stands between you and a right
  relationship with God? Confess it and find favor
  once again.

- We often go through these seasons of night, but they don't last forever. Seasons come and go as winter moves to spring. Sometimes it seems like forever, but nothing lasts in this world. Joy will come in the morning, often when we least expect it. If we're not careful, we can miss the little joys of life while we're waiting. There is joy in small accomplishments, laughter, and rainbows on a cloudy day. What are some little joys God has sent your way today?

Father, thank You for what You have done in my life. Thank You for Your holiness. Sometimes I stray from the path, but You are faithful to take me back in love and return me to Your favor. I know there will be dark times in this life, but You promise that they won't last forever. Give me strength to endure the night, and help me to be thankful for the joy that will come when the night is over.

Not Forgotten

I cried unto God with my voice, even unto God
with my voice; and he gave ear unto me. In the
day of my trouble I sought the Lord: my sore ran
in the night, and ceased not: my soul refused to be
comforted. I remembered God, and was troubled: I
complained, and my spirit was overwhelmed. Selah.

PSALM 77:1–3

- Have you ever felt forgotten by God? Did your troubles seem so overwhelming that you felt abandoned? Asaph, the writer of this psalm, was in deep distress and cried out for help. In the first nine verses he lays his complaint before God with an emphasis on "I." Asaph complained to God and was troubled because he didn't see God moving on his behalf. Are you overcome by troubles and wondering where God is?

- In verse ten of this chapter Asaph begins to recall what God has done in the past. He recalls the wonders and works of God and begins to meditate on that instead of his troubles. Sometimes we need a shift in focus. If we're anxious and dwell on the anxiety, it merely increases. However, if we find another focus, it helps to alleviate the anxiety. While the issue may not disappear, it is lightened. What has God done for you in the past? What is He doing in your life right now?

- Asaph spends the rest of the chapter talking about God and praising Him for His greatness. How did he go from complaining to praising? He changed his focus. When we meditate on the Word of God, the problems of the world fade in comparison. While the troubles may not be gone, they are put in perspective. Are you overwhelmed? Tell God your troubles and then meditate on the scriptures. You might be surprised at what a difference a change in focus can do for your spirit.

Father, I am drowning under troubles, and I don't see a way out. I feel forgotten and wonder where You are. Then, I remember Your mercies and all the works You have done in my life. I praise You for Your mighty works, and I am believing for You to do it again. Help me change my focus and see You at work in my situation. I praise Your name, for it is holy, and I thank You that I am not forgotten.

The Journey

But made his own people to go forth like sheep,
and guided them in the wilderness like a flock. And
he led them on safely, so that they feared not: but
the sea overwhelmed their enemies. And he brought
them to the border of his sanctuary, even to this
mountain, which his right hand had purchased.

PSALM 78:52–54

- Have you ever felt like you were in the wilderness? The psalmist is recalling how God called His people out of Egypt and took them through the wilderness to the promised land. The Christian life is a journey to a different promised land: heaven. This life is often like a wilderness that we must navigate through, but there is joy in the journey. What are some highlights of your journey so far?

- As the children of Israel made their way through the desert, God guided them like a flock of sheep and protected them day and night so that they safely reached the border. We too are watched over by our Shepherd, Jesus Christ. How have you seen the Shepherd at work protecting you?

- When the Israelites reached the border, God performed a mighty miracle. He parted the waters so they passed on dry land, but their enemies were overwhelmed by the sea. In our journey, God is defeating our enemies as we travel along— sometimes in miraculous ways and sometimes in subtle ways. What enemies have you seen defeated? How did God make it happen?

- God bought our freedom through the blood of His Son, Jesus, His right hand. His sacrifice purchased us a place in His sanctuary. He is ever leading us to His mountain and the border of the promised land. Someday when we cross into heaven, we will cross the river, but our enemy death will be overwhelmed by God's grace. We have nothing to fear from the journey because it merely is the way to our eternal home with God. What do you look forward to at journey's end?

Father, thank You for calling us out of sin and into Your glorious light. You are leading us through the wilderness to the promised land, and one day we will live eternally in Your sanctuary. In the meantime, thank You for Your protection from our earthly enemies as we journey onward and for defeating the enemy of death so that we have nothing to fear.

Everlasting Foundation

*Of old hast thou laid the foundation of the earth:
and the heavens are the work of thy hands. They
shall perish, but thou shalt endure: yea, all of them
shall wax old like a garment; as a vesture shalt thou
change them, and they shall be changed: but thou
art the same, and thy years shall have no end.*

PSALM 102:25–27

- God laid the foundations of the earth, but the
  Bible tells us that one day it will pass away. When
  sin entered the picture, it started a domino effect
  of degeneration. Revelation tells us that one day
  there will be a new heaven and a new earth where
  we will be for eternity. Yet while the creation will
  be destroyed and re-created, the Creator has not
  and will not change. He is eternal. In this world
  there is constant change, but we can depend on
  one thing: God doesn't change. What is changing
  in your life? Do you hold on to the constancy of
  God during times of change?

- Have you ever had a favorite article of clothing
  that slowly degraded over time? Our lives are the
  same way because these bodies will deteriorate as
  we age, but we too will be renewed so that we can
  live eternally with God.

- Do you watch the news or drive through your town and see constant changes being made? Technology advances alone are enough to make your head spin as new changes come out every year. Do you feel overwhelmed by all the changes? Then hold on to the truth that even when the foundations are shaken, God will not be moved. He is an everlasting foundation, and on that you can rely.

Father, I see the changes all around me, and some are not for the better. The world seems to be getting colder and darker every day as Your approach draws nearer, but I'm thankful that I can depend on You not to change. You are the same yesterday, today, and forevermore. Praise be to God!

If Not for the Lord

If it had not been the LORD who was on our side,
now may Israel say; if it had not been the LORD
who was on our side, when men rose up against us:
then they had swallowed us up quick, when their
wrath was kindled against us: then the waters had
overwhelmed us, the stream had gone over our soul.

PSALM 124:1–4

- Have you ever noticed the power of repetition? Consider Martin Luther King Jr.'s "I Have a Dream" speech. There is power in the repetition of the phrase "I have a dream." The Bible writers also used this technique when they wanted to emphasize a point. In these verses, the psalmist is emphasizing what would happen if not for the Lord being on our side.

- The psalmist is reminding Israel what would have happened if God had not defended them against their enemies. If not for God, they would have been swallowed by the wrath of enemy nations. We're likely not fighting an enemy nation, but sometimes we feel attacked by stress or anxiety. If it weren't for God, we would have been swallowed up by it. What are you fighting? How has God been on your side?

- The psalmist goes on to say they would have drowned if the Lord had not intervened. Do you sometimes feel like you are drowning in debt or fear or loss? God is still on your side. If you call on Him, He will keep you from being overwhelmed by the flood.

- If not for the Lord, where would you be? What has God done for you that only He could do?

Father, if it had not been for You and the sacrifice of Your Son, I don't know where I would be right now. I'm thankful for Your grace, mercy, and love that never cease. I am even more thankful for salvation and the forgiveness of sin so that I can be in a right relationship with You as an adopted child with all the benefits and privileges that brings. I'm thankful that I don't have to worry about where I would be without You on my side. Praise God!

My Portion

*When my spirit was overwhelmed within me, then
thou knewest my path. In the way wherein I walked
have they privily laid a snare for me. I looked on my
right hand, and beheld, but there was no man that
would know me: refuge failed me; no man cared for
my soul. I cried unto thee, O LORD: I said, Thou art
my refuge and my portion in the land of the living.*

PSALM 142:3–5

- This psalm was written while David was hiding
  in a cave. Think about that for a minute. Have
  you ever had to take prolonged shelter in a cave
  because someone was trying to kill you? Whenever
  we are whining too much, God can bring to mind
  people who are in dire circumstances. It helps to
  have a little perspective. When has God given you
  perspective on your situation?

- David starts out by saying that God knew his heart
  and his location. God was not uninformed. Saul
  had laid traps for David everywhere, and nobody
  wanted to help him for fear of Saul, so he was forced
  to hide in a cave. He had no other place to go. Have
  you ever felt like there was no one you could turn
  to, no refuge to run to?

- David turned to his only hope. He turned to God and cried out for help. Even in those dire straits, David knew where to go because he had made a habit of maintaining a relationship with God throughout his life. He had defended his sheep against lions and bears and even defeated Goliath, but not without the help of God. Where do you turn first when you run into trouble?

- David knew that God, not the cave, was his real refuge. God would protect him from Saul because he had already been anointed as king. He chose God as his portion even though the circumstances were hard. Is God your portion?

Father, when it seems like I have nowhere to go and no one to turn to, I can turn to You. You are a refuge in times of trouble, but You are also my portion every day. Thank You for Your presence and Your protection when the enemy seeks to destroy me. I know I can depend on You even if all else fails me. You truly are my refuge.

The Hope of the Solitary

A father of the fatherless, and a judge of the widows,
is God in his holy habitation. God setteth the solitary
in families: he bringeth out those which are bound
with chains: but the rebellious dwell in a dry land.

PSALM 68:5–6

- Have you ever felt alone in the world? Many times it's just a feeling of not being understood, but for people in David's time, being solitary was hard and sometimes dangerous. There were no public programs to help the orphans, and widows couldn't simply go get a job. If another family didn't take them in, they were left to beg in the streets or glean the leftovers in the fields. However, God was a Father to the orphan and a judge of how the widows were treated. We are never truly alone.

- Not only does God see the plight of the solitary, but He puts them in families. One of God's commands to the church is to help the widows and orphans, but really it's about helping all the marginalized in society. God built us to be in community and to be a community to those who have no one. Is there someone you can bring into your church family who is alone?

- God also freed those who were bound by chains, whether in servitude or in prison. Many were imprisoned for owing money or because they were sold into slavery by their family due to poverty. But it is also those who are enslaved to sin. God sent His only Son to be a sacrifice so that we could all be set free from sin and adopted into a family. There are many in our midst who are alone and need our help. How can you reach out to those who are lost in your community?

Father, even when I feel alone, You are always there. You are the hope of the solitary, the widows and orphans, and those who are in chains. You have made a way for all to get to heaven and adopted them as Your own, but I am also responsible for helping the lonely. It is the job of the church and individual Christians to take the solitary into the family of God. Show me how I can be Your hands and feet in my community. Help me see them with Your eyes of love.

My Expectation Is from God

*My soul, wait thou only upon God; for my
expectation is from him. He only is my rock and my
salvation: he is my defence; I shall not be moved.*

PSALM 62:5–6

- Where do you go when you're in trouble? When you were little, you probably ran to a parent or grandparent to fix a scratched knee or hurt feelings. As an adult, where do you go?

- George Müller was a missionary in Bristol, England, where an outbreak of a cholera epidemic had left many orphans. He started numerous orphanages based solely on trust in God. He never asked for funding, but he was able to house, clothe, and feed countless children. He said his expectation came from God alone and felt led never to ask others for anything but to lay his cause before the Lord. His prayers were always answered, although sometimes at the eleventh hour. Do you wait on God, or do you try to take care of it yourself?

- Think of all the stories throughout the Bible of people like Abraham and Sarah who tried to make things happen on their own. Do you ever try to force God's work into your timeline? It never turns out well. Have you tried to make something happen, only to have it go wrong? You may never know what might have happened if you had waited on God.

- David was a warrior and a king, but even he said that God was his rock, salvation, and defense. David knew the only way he would win was to follow God's leadership and wait for Him to move. He waited years for his anointing as king to become final so that he could take the throne, but God blessed him and his reign. What are you waiting for? Are you waiting on God's timing?

Father, I'm often impatient and desire to be self-sufficient, but I know that things work out better when You work out the details. Help me to lean on You and let my expectation come only from You. It's a daily battle, but I know You have my best interest at heart. I will trust You because You alone are my rock, my salvation, and my defense.

Joy over Us with Singing

The LORD thy God in the midst of thee is mighty;
he will save, he will rejoice over thee with joy; he will
rest in his love, he will joy over thee with singing.

ZEPHANIAH 3:17

- Zephaniah was a prophet to Israel. He reminded them that God would remove His hand of judgment if they would return to Him. The first thing Zephaniah noted was that God was still in the midst of them, waiting. Have you wandered away from God's will for your life? If you turn back, He will welcome you with open arms.

- The second thing he pointed out was that the God in the midst of them was mighty enough to save them from their troubles. It's easy to get caught up in our circumstances and feel like there is no way out, but God can make a way. Think of the Israelites at the Red Sea. It looked like a dead end, but God rolled the water back so that they crossed on dry land, and then He let it fall on their enemies and destroy them. What is it you need God to do for you?

- Zephaniah then said God will rejoice over you. It brings God great joy when His children return to Him. He will share that joy with you as well. Have you ever felt the joy of the Lord over your life?

- Not only does God rejoice over us, but His love is a resting place for our souls. If you truly want peace in your life no matter what the circumstances, then you must draw close to God, who is the source of joy. Do you need rest for your soul? Then get closer to God through prayer and singing His praises.

- Finally, He will rejoice over you with singing. Can you imagine that? God sings over us! We are His children, and He sings over us. How does it feel to know that God is singing over your soul?

Father, I'm thankful that You are here with me. You are mighty, and You have saved me by Your grace. I want to be close to You and feel Your joy, love, and singing. Help me to stay close so that I can rest in Your love and know that You rejoice over me with singing.

Peace of Mind

Thou wilt keep him in perfect peace, whose mind
is stayed on thee: because he trusteth in thee.

ISAIAH 26:3

- When was the last time you had perfect peace? In this world it's hard to do, but it is not impossible. What do you have to do to achieve it? It's really a matter of focus and trust.

- Who will keep you in perfect peace? God will. It's not something that we do ourselves, because we don't have that power. We may be able to achieve a moment of peace, but perfect, complete peace is not humanly possible. We are easily led astray by all the distractions and noise of the world, but God can give it to us.

- How do we get perfect peace? We keep our minds stayed on God. Can we do this constantly? Probably not, but when our minds are focused on God and not the world, we have a right perspective and right relationship with God, which results in peace. What is distracting you today? When the world crashes in, open your Bible and read the Word of God, sing praises, or just talk to your Father. These are ways you can put your focus back in the right direction.

- Perfect peace is the result of trusting God. When we trust God, then we don't worry about what is going on around us. If you believe God is in control of all situations, then you can let go of trying to handle it yourself, and you can let go of the worry associated with it. Think of a task at work that you had no idea how you could accomplish. What does it feel like when someone comes along and takes it off your list and takes care of it without belittling you? You can relax. You have peace. God wants to take care of your situation, but you have to let go of it. Once you do, the result is peace of mind.

Father, this world is chaotic, and people are at odds with each other every way I turn. I want the peace that only You can give. Help me to keep my mind stayed on You, for I know that the only way to have peace is to focus on You and not on my circumstances. Help me to trust You more, because that is the way to true peace for my mind, heart, spirit, and body.

Don't Worry; Just Pray

*Be careful for nothing; but in every thing by prayer
and supplication with thanksgiving let your
requests be made known unto God. And the peace
of God, which passeth all understanding, shall keep
your hearts and minds through Christ Jesus.*

PHILIPPIANS 4:6–7

- Do you worry? It's probably a silly question, because
  everyone worries about something sometimes. The
  main thing is not to make it a habit, because it steals
  the joy of today while you stress over something
  that hasn't even happened yet. What are some ways
  you can break the habit of worry?

- Paul gave a simple answer to the question in his
  letter to the Philippians. "Be careful for nothing"
  could be translated *don't worry about anything*. But
  he doesn't stop there. He gives practical advice for
  how to cut worry out of the equation: pray. Instead
  of worrying about something you probably can't
  change, tell God about it. What is worrying you
  today?

- So, how do we pray? We should start with thanksgiving. Sometimes just listing all the wonderful
  things God has done not only shows our gratitude
  but reminds us of what God is capable of and has

already completed. Next, humbly make your requests known. God is not a vending machine who gives us what we demand. He is a loving God who wants to take care of us, and He is still God and deserves our respect. What are you thankful for today?

- What is the final result? The peace of God, which passes all understanding, will replace the worry. When we take on the mind of Christ Jesus, then we are in sync with what God wants to do. If you remember all that God has done for you and trust Him with your heart, then you can lay your worries at His feet and pick up peace in exchange. Can you think of a better exchange program? Don't worry; just pray.

Father, I know I worry too much. Today, I lift up my requests to You, thanking You for Your gift of salvation and grace. Thank You for answering my prayers. I know that You are in control and have my best interests at heart, so I leave my worries here with You, and I ask for the peace that passeth all understanding, which only comes from You.

Pay Your Vows

*Offer unto God thanksgiving; and pay thy vows unto
the most High: and call upon me in the day of trouble:
I will deliver thee, and thou shalt glorify me.*

PSALM 50:14–15

- Many people read these verses and skip the section
  in the middle about paying vows. How does this
  work? Well, consider when you borrow money
  from the bank. You sign a contract saying you will
  pay back the money in a series of payments by a
  set time. If you are late, they will send warnings.
  Eventually, if you don't pay it back, there will be
  consequences. While God is more forgiving than
  the bank, there are consequences to not paying your
  vows to Him. Have you promised God you would do
  something but have not followed through?

- Asaph, the psalmist, wrote this psalm about
  the contrast between true and false faith. True
  believers are thankful to God for all the things He
  has done and follow through on what they vow to
  do. The world is full of people who say one thing and
  do another. We call them hypocrites or two-faced,
  but what happens when we do the same thing?
  Christians are different from the world because
  they do what they say.

- When you're in trouble, you want to be able to go to God with a clear conscience to ask for help. Sometimes the answers to prayer don't come until we follow through on our part. So, paying our vows is important both to our witness and to our relationship with God.

- Another sign of a true believer comes when they are delivered out of trouble. Who gets the glory when God answers your prayer? Does God, or do you give yourself or someone else credit? God is the one who is worthy of our thanks and our praise, so make it a priority to give credit where credit is due. Not only is this pleasing to God, but it is a good witness to the world that true believers are different from the world.

Father, when I'm overwhelmed by trouble, I come to You for deliverance. I'm thankful for all the prayers You answered. Because of that, I will pay my vows and follow through on what I have promised to do. Then I will give You the glory for answered prayers.

Hope in Believing

Now the God of hope fill you with all joy and peace in believing, that ye may abound in hope, through the power of the Holy Ghost.

ROMANS 15:13

- Have you ever lost hope? Have the world and circumstances crushed your spirit? Hope can still be found if you know the right place to look for it. Where is that place in your life?

- In Romans 15:13, Paul is praying to God for the church as he is closing out his letter to the Romans. He addresses his prayer to the "God of hope," which is a reminder that our hope is built on God as our foundation. Any other hope is fleeting and deceitful. What have you placed your hope in?

- Paul prays that the church will be filled with joy in God and peace in their conscience because of what Christ had done for them. Joy and peace promote unity and fellowship within the believers as a congregation, but they also are a firm foundation for hope in the individual. We have hope because of our position in Christ. Have you lost your joy and peace? Follow Paul's example and ask God, the giver of good gifts, to fill you.

- What are you hoping for? Joy and peace are tied to hope. The more hope we have, the more joy and peace we will have, but the hope is not one of earthly things but one of great things from God—the kind of things that you can only receive through the power of the Holy Spirit.

- How do you find hope? First, go to the source and ask to be filled with joy and peace. Pray to the God of hope. Next, read the Bible and remember your source of hope is Christ's sacrifice on the cross, which gives you access to a personal relationship with God and a home in heaven. Finally, hope for the things that last—things that only the Holy Spirit can give. Then, you will have a hope everlasting, the kind that only comes through believing.

Father, it's easy to lose hope in this world when I'm surrounded by chaos and confusion, but I know that the true source of hope is You. Fill me with Your joy and peace so that I may abound in hope. My only real hope is believing in Your Son and all He has done for me.

World's Greatest Dad

My sheep hear my voice, and I know them, and they follow me: and I give unto them eternal life; and they shall never perish, neither shall any man pluck them out of my hand. My Father, which gave them me, is greater than all; and no man is able to pluck them out of my Father's hand. I and my Father are one.

JOHN 10:27–30

- Has anyone, a sibling or bully maybe, taken something out of your hand and played keep-away? It's frustrating and aggravating at the very least, but sometimes it can be scary, depending on what was taken. Usually, it requires someone bigger than the perpetrator to come in and take it back and restore the item to its owner. Sometimes the bigger person is a dad who comes in with authority and strength to bring justice. Many people will claim they have the world's greatest dad, but we have a heavenly Father who tops them all.

- While not everyone has a loving earthly father, as Christians we have a heavenly Father who calls us to follow Him. When we make that decision to follow Christ, we belong to God, and His voice becomes familiar to us, because Jesus and our heavenly Father are one.

- Are you afraid of the future? Of death? These verses tell us that once we choose Christ we are in His hands, and nothing can pluck us out of them. Our heavenly Father is the greatest and strongest. We have nothing to fear from the world or eternity. We are safely held in the palm of the world's greatest Dad, and no one can touch us.

Father, You are truly the greatest Father in heaven and earth. You are powerful, but You are also loving and kind. You watch over us, protect us, and provide for us. I long to know Your voice better and to follow You wherever You may lead. I'm thankful that no one can pluck me from Your loving hand. I praise You for Your Father's heart and everlasting love for me, Your beloved daughter.

Grab Your Sword

(For the weapons of our warfare are not carnal,
but mighty through God to the pulling down of
strong holds;) casting down imaginations, and
every high thing that exalteth itself against the
knowledge of God, and bringing into captivity
every thought to the obedience of Christ.

2 CORINTHIANS 10:4–5

- Did you know we are at war? Every day we face a spiritual battle against the enemy in the physical world. It can seem like we will never win, especially when the enemy adds his schemes and plans into the mix. Do you feel as if you do the things you shouldn't and don't do the things you should? It's a common problem for all humans; however, we have a weapon.

- The Word of God is our weapon against all attacks because it is backed by the power of the Holy Spirit. It's mighty enough to pull down strongholds or a place of power. Spiritually speaking, it can be an area of our life the enemy has made us believe that we can never overcome. Yet, these verses say that God's Word is mighty to overcome anything. Is there a stronghold in your spiritual life that you need to take back?

- How do we use our weapon? First, we need to throw down anything that we exalt above God. It's easy to allow things of this world to take priority in our life, but we need to identify anything that is taking more of our time or thoughts. Second, we have to intentionally work at taking those thoughts and things captive so that we are obedient to Christ.

- There will always be a war, so we need to stand ready to protect our hearts against attacks of the enemy. The way to do that is to be immersed in the Word of God. It's not just daily Bible reading but studying and digging into the application of the scriptures to our everyday lives. So, grab your Sword and start practicing so that you can take down strongholds and deepen your walk with God.

Father, I pray that You would help me wield the weapon of Your Word. I know there are areas that I struggle with, so I ask You to help me identify them and show me what I need to do to take back those areas of my life from the enemy. Help me as I battle against the thoughts that wage war inside of me and replace them with Your Word.

Conflict of Interest

This I say then, Walk in the Spirit, and ye shall not fulfil the lust of the flesh. For the flesh lusteth against the Spirit, and the Spirit against the flesh: and these are contrary the one to the other: so that ye cannot do the things that ye would.

GALATIANS 5:16–17

- Paul is writing to the church at Galatia about practical godliness as an antidote to false teachers. In this section Paul emphasizes the need to focus on battling the sin in our own lives to promote not only godliness but also unity in the church. If each person minded their own spiritual condition, they wouldn't have time to argue, and they would be more compassionate to one another since the battle is common to everyone. Are there things you know you should do but don't? Are there things you shouldn't do but do?

- The spiritual person and the physical person within us always have a conflict of interest. The physical person follows the lust of the flesh, while the spiritual person follows after the Spirit. We choose which one we allow to win, but first we have to identify that there is a conflict. Like most conflicts, we also have to choose a side. Which side do you want to identify with?

- We must be intentional in not only choosing a side but also supporting it. How do you walk in the Spirit? You have to make sure to deepen your relationship with the Holy Spirit through Bible study, prayer, and worship. Even then, it is a day-to-day battle. So, every morning, try inviting the Holy Spirit into your life for that day. He will guide you like a general as you navigate the day's events and temptations.

- When we leave these physical bodies behind, we will be free of the conflict. In the meantime, we have our fearless leader to help us fight the daily battles. Some we will win, and some we will lose, but God is faithful to forgive us when we ask.

Father, I'm in a daily battle to do what is right. I want to walk in Your way, but I need Your help to fight the enemy inside of me. Show me where I need improvement and help me know how to guard against potential stumbling blocks. Holy Spirit, please come.

An Expected End

*For I know the thoughts that I think toward
you, saith the LORD, thoughts of peace, and
not of evil, to give you an expected end.*

JEREMIAH 29:11

- Jeremiah wanted the people who had been taken captive into Babylon to know that though God had allowed it, He had not forgotten His people. This verse is not a promise to always be in a prosperous place; it is a reminder that there is hope no matter what your circumstances. Are you overwhelmed by your circumstances? Don't give up, because the God of hope is still on your side.

- God is a leader who stirs us to move forward believing we can do whatever tasks He has called us to because He has also equipped us. He has a plan, He knows what is coming, and He is always with us, so we can have hope for a future. Have you lost hope? Just remember that God is with you in your circumstances and is walking beside you.

- There will always be troubles in this world, and they come to everyone. All of our circumstances are temporary, good or bad. We move through seasons and cycles, but there is an expected end, both to the season and to this life. We have a hope in this world, but we also have an even greater hope in eternity. How is God at work in your circumstances?

- False teachers were working in Jeremiah's day, telling the people what they wanted to hear instead of the truth. They told them that God would defeat all their enemies and they would be saved, but they ended up in captivity in Babylon. We have hope even if circumstances aren't exactly what we wanted. Have people been telling you what you want to hear? Make sure that you are listening to individuals who are tapped into the power of the Holy Spirit and are not afraid to tell you the truth.

Father, I'm weary of my circumstances, but I know that You are here beside me. You will use these events for my good if I will follow Your purpose in my life. Give me discernment so that I can tell the difference between false teachers and those who profess the truth. Send Your peace through the Holy Spirit so that even in tough times I can rest in the hope that this season will come to an expected end.

Your Best Defense

No weapon that is formed against thee shall
prosper; and every tongue that shall rise against
thee in judgment thou shalt condemn. This is
the heritage of the servants of the LORD, and
their righteousness is of me, saith the LORD.

ISAIAH 54:17

- This verse is a description of God's promise of safety
  to the children of Israel and to the future church.
  He is our defender and will protect us from our
  enemies; however, that does not mean that we
  will never suffer trials and tribulations. It means
  that on God's timetable He will make everything
  work for the good of His people and bring justice against our enemies. Are you worried by the
  state of the world? We don't have to be afraid
  because God is our defense.

- The children of Israel and the church have different
  kinds of enemies. But Isaiah 54:17 says no weapons
  formed against God's people will prosper. That
  doesn't mean there won't be persecution, but it
  does mean that they won't win in the end. Have
  you been falsely accused or persecuted because
  of your beliefs?

- Has anyone ever lied about you or accused you unjustly? We may suffer unrighteous attacks just as Jesus did, but God will reward those who suffer, and He will use it for our overall good. God is faithful and just, but He works on His own schedule. We just have to rest in the knowledge that He will be our best defense, and He will reward those who are faithful to Him.

Father, I'm surrounded by a culture that is offended by Christianity and seeks to silence my testimony, but I know You are at work defending me for Your name's sake. I know I will probably suffer trials and difficulties for my beliefs, and people will rise up and speak lies against me. Help me to respond in love and peace, knowing that You will take care of the end results for my good. I'm thankful You are my defender.

Promise of Restoration

*Who is a God like unto thee, that pardoneth iniquity,
and passeth by the transgression of the remnant of
his heritage? he retaineth not his anger for ever,
because he delighteth in mercy. He will turn again,
he will have compassion upon us; he will subdue
our iniquities; and thou wilt cast all their sins into
the depths of the sea. Thou wilt perform the truth
to Jacob, and the mercy to Abraham, which thou
hast sworn unto our fathers from the days of old.*

MICAH 7:18–20

- Have you ever slipped into sin and wondered if God could ever forgive you? Good news! God is a merciful God who seeks to reconcile us to Himself. He wants a right relationship with us and is willing to restore us if we ask and repent. The flip side is that God also expects the same behavior from us. In a world that is unfair, unjust, and proud, we must act justly, be merciful, and be humble.

- We have reason to rejoice and give God the glory for His pardoning mercy. It is the foundation of all the covenant mercies because without pardon of sin, none of the other forms of mercy would matter. Even though the remnant of His heritage is filled with sinners, God still gives forgiveness in exchange for repentance, and His righteous anger doesn't last forever. He delights in the salvation of sinners. Isn't that something to rejoice over?

- Will you slip again? Yes, because we all sin and are in need of mercy and forgiveness. So, we can rejoice for His forgiveness in the past, but we can also look forward to the assurance of renewed mercies in the future. God is always the same, so if He did it before, He will do it again.

- How great is the grace of God? He breaks the power of sin by giving us a pardon that can never be repealed by any court. He has the final say. He is faithful to fulfill His covenant, so we can depend on this foundational truth.

Father, how great is Your mercy and faithfulness to me, a sinner. Even though I'm constantly stumbling, You are faithful to restore me to a right relationship with You when I ask for forgiveness— and not just once. Over and over again You have shown me mercy, so I thank You and praise You.

Change Your Thinking

*Finally, brethren, whatsoever things are true,
whatsoever things are honest, whatsoever
things are just, whatsoever things are pure,
whatsoever things are lovely, whatsoever things
are of good report; if there be any virtue, and if
there be any praise, think on these things.*

PHILIPPIANS 4:8

- In computer programming the computer will only output what you input. If we want to change our outlook, we have to change our input. A new attitude starts with changing the way you think. What do you find yourself thinking about most during the day? Is it past hurts, current circumstances, or worries of the future? Maybe all those swirling around in chaos? How does that affect your mood and attitude?

- The scripture gives guidance on what types of things we should be focused on in order to have peace and joy. First, we should think only of things that are true and honest so that we can be truthful and honest in our dealings with others. What are some truths you can think on? The scripture is our go-to for divining what is true. If you do not have hard evidence of something, then don't dwell on it or repeat it.

- We should also think about things that are just and pure and allow that to flow over into our dealings with people. When we think on things that are lovely and of good report, we are more likely to be amiable and better company. Have you ever been in a group that is discussing the most current perceived injustice in their lives or the world? What is the attitude of the group? On the other hand, what happens when people share good news or even just a lighthearted story? Whatever we focus on will eventually affect our attitude and behavior.

- If we want to be a good representative of God, then we should try each day to be more like Jesus. It all starts with our thinking. What are some ways you can spend more time inputting goodness and truth?

Father, this world is full of negativity and anger. It's contagious. Help me to find ways to avoid prolonged interaction with things that take my focus off what is true, honest, just, pure, lovely, of good report, virtuous, and praiseworthy. Help me to put in the kinds of things that will create a right attitude and spirit in me so that I can be an example of Christ in the world.

Renewal in Waiting

*But they that wait upon the L*ORD *shall renew their strength; they shall mount up with wings as eagles; they shall run, and not be weary; and they shall walk, and not faint.*

ISAIAH 40:31

- Do you like waiting? Our culture is always in a hurry to check off their list and keep busy. People are proud and feel self-sufficient. They don't need God or anyone else to help them get where they are going. The problem is that people do not have an unlimited supply of energy. Eventually, they will burn out and hit bottom. Have you ever been there?

- What's the alternative? The solution is a different approach to our daily lives: renewal through waiting. It's not the waiting-in-line kind of waiting. Waiting, meaning relying on God's power instead of your own. He has unlimited energy available for the asking, but it requires admitting that you are not self-sufficient. It also means waiting for Him to move instead of trying to do everything ourselves.

- Should we just be lazy and wait for God to do everything? No. It's a lifestyle that recognizes our limitations as we go about our assigned tasks. If we do our part and rely on God to help us, He will renew our strength continually. God will not bless laziness, but He also will not bless self-sufficiency. However, He will bless a humble spirit.

- Are you tired of always being on the run? Then turn to the Lord. When we are aware of our need for God and by faith commit ourselves to His leading, God will not fail us. He is faithful to follow through on His promises, even though sometimes we may have to wait. But in the waiting is a rest that is a renewal to our bodies and our spirits. Are you ready to wait on the Lord so that you can soar like the eagles?

Father, I'm tired of running on my own strength. I need Your power to lift and renew me. Help me to wait on You and Your timing and to rely on Your strength to complete the tasks You have given me. My burdens are lighter when I am yoked with You. I want to mount upon wings like eagles, but I need You to lift me. Renew my strength as only You can.

Steady On

Rejoice evermore. Pray without ceasing. In every thing give thanks: for this is the will of God in Christ Jesus concerning you. Quench not the Spirit.

1 THESSALONIANS 5:16–19

- Do you ever feel like someone has pulled the rug out from under your feet? Maybe a relationship or a job ends. Suddenly your world is in chaos, and you can't find your footing. We have all had times when we felt like we were spinning out of control, so what can we do to keep steady, even in times of turmoil? Paul gives a list of ways in 1 Thessalonians 5:16–19 that we can maintain our balance even when the world around us is shaking.

- How do you rejoice evermore? Does that mean that's all you do all day? Actually, it's a spiritual joy that is always with us because of our salvation and the presence of the Holy Spirit. It's "evermore" or everlasting because our salvation is eternal, not temporal. Just being aware of the presence of God is joy in itself. When you have joy, it changes your perspective.

- How do you pray without ceasing? What does that do? Prayer is simply a conversation with God the Father. We never close the lines of communication.

It's always available. We can keep a prayerful attitude that results in short bursts of prayer, but we should also have those longer talks that include thanksgiving and intercessory prayer as well as confession. When we keep the lines open, we know we have access to help at any time.

- Should we be thankful for everything? Not everything is sent from God, so it's more about giving thanks *in* everything but not *for* everything. When we lose someone we love, we are not thankful that they are dead, but we are thankful for God's presence during our time of loss. Again, it is a change in our perspective.

- How do you quench the Spirit? The Holy Spirit is quenched when we indulge in carnal lusts or mind only the things of earth. To keep the fire burning, we must stir up the Spirit like a campfire to keep it burning. When we focus on the things of God, then we keep the Spirit flowing.

- If we follow these commands, then in times of crisis or upheaval we can keep moving steady on because our focus is on the eternal that never changes.

Father, help me keep my focus on You through joy, prayer, thanksgiving, and my spirit. Help me to move steady on as I focus on You.

What If?

Therefore take no thought, saying, What shall we eat? or, What shall we drink? or, Wherewithal shall we be clothed? (For after all these things do the Gentiles seek:) for your heavenly Father knoweth that ye have need of all these things. But seek ye first the kingdom of God, and his righteousness; and all these things shall be added unto you. Take therefore no thought for the morrow: for the morrow shall take thought for the things of itself. Sufficient unto the day is the evil thereof.

MATTHEW 6:31–34

- What if? Those two little words can send us spiraling downward in fear and anxiety. Do you worry about finances and the future? Does it leave you frozen in your tracks? The good news is that God knows your needs and is ready to provide for them.

- The world is always stressed out about what comes next. Even when they're not worried about whether or not they have clothes to wear, they worry about which clothes to wear to impress the right people or to fit in with the crowd. How do you break out of this cycle?

- The scripture says take no thought, but that phrase can also be translated "be not in care." We have to be responsible in planning a budget and trying to make the best use of what we have been given, but planning is different from the kind of thoughts mentioned here. If it's a tormenting thought that is distracting, disturbing peace and joy, or distrustful, then it is not of God. What kind of thought is useful?

- Seeking the things of God means going to God first instead of worrying. Worry is a sign that we don't trust God, and it's a sin. When we take our needs to God and leave them in His hands, then we can continue on with our duties in peace.

- What about tomorrow? What if tomorrow never comes? The truth is we don't know how long we have on this earth. Your situation could change in an instant for better or worse. All we can do is plan based on what we know and be flexible as the days unfold.

Father, worry brings me nothing but stress and fear. You are trustworthy, and You tell me that when I bring my needs to You, You will provide for me. Help me to plan so that my duties are done and to rely on You to handle tomorrow.

Supply and Demand

*But my God shall supply all your need according
to his riches in glory by Christ Jesus.*

PHILIPPIANS 4:19

- Have you ever asked God for something, and He
  said no? False teachers have declared that if you
  name it and claim it, it is yours; God will grant you
  whatever you ask if you just have enough faith. We
  demand, and He supplies. But God is not a vending
  machine, though He is a caring Father. Sometimes
  we ask for things that aren't good for us or will
  hurt us down the road. So, when Paul says God will
  supply all your needs, what did he mean?

- Paul spends the earlier part of the chapter thanking
  the Philippian church for supplying his needs.
  Here he is saying that God would respond in kind
  to them and take care of their needs. But what do
  we mean when we say *need*?

- Many people confuse needs with wants. It's only in
  times of crisis that we really see what are needs and
  what are wants. Have you ever gone in the grocery
  store with a limited amount of cash at your disposal
  and a shopping list, only to realize that you don't
  have enough money for everything on the list?
  Maybe you review the list and determine what can

wait another week or is not really necessary. God loves us so much that He is more concerned with our needs, yet He often blesses us with our wants as well. The key word there is *blesses*.

- Have you ever ordered something, and it didn't come on time? Were you frustrated? Sometimes we have to wait for God's timing. When we pray, we often expect immediate answers, but sometimes God sends the answer just in time to help build our faith so that He gets the glory. Sometimes we need to wait because God has something far greater than we asked for.

- What do you have need of today? Humbly take it to the Father and ask, knowing that God will provide for all our needs in His own way and His own time, but He is faithful to do what He says.

Father, You know my needs even better than I do, but I humbly lift this request to You. I thank You for Your provision as I wait in faith for You to work in Your will and way.

Don't Stir the Pot

A soft answer turneth away wrath:
but grievous words stir up anger.

PROVERBS 15:1

- Have you ever made a recipe that required constant stirring? Usually, it's to keep things hot and boiling without sticking. Other recipes are better if you leave them alone. For instance, if you turn a pancake too quickly, you can have a mess. The key is to know when not to stir the pot.

- We can become overwhelmed by the anger and violence of our world, but Proverbs is a book of wisdom for everyday life. It was written by King Solomon, who was considered one of the wisest men of his time. It's full of common sense that can make life easier if we will take the time to read and apply it. In a culture that is always at odds, this particular piece of advice could go a long way to bringing peace to our world. What is a soft answer?

- Have you ever been in a group where someone brings up a hot topic, like politics, and suddenly a calm discussion turns into a screaming match? When we disagree with someone, our attitude and choice of words can go a long way to defusing a potentially volatile situation. A soft answer is a voice of calm logic that tries to understand the other person's position. If the other person is yelling and you raise your voice, it will only lead to escalation. So, if we take a breath and speak calmly, we have a better chance of settling things amicably.

- What are grievous words? Using insults or trying to intimidate people are the kinds of things that are grievous to people. They stir up anger and a need to defend, which only leads to more anger. It only takes one person being willing to speak gently to turn the tide of the argument.

- Are you willing to be a voice of calm and peace in a world full of anger? Jesus is our example of how to deal with opponents. He spoke calmly and used the scriptures and parables to make His point. Often, He merely asked questions. Time and again in the New Testament, His gentle spirit brought peace where others meant to bring division.

Father, may we be a soft voice in a loud world. May we follow Jesus' example in dealing with those who seek to cause division and anger. Help us to be messengers of peace and love so that You may be glorified.

The Waiting

I had fainted, unless I had believed to see the
goodness of the LORD in the land of the living.
Wait on the LORD: be of good courage, and he shall
strengthen thine heart: wait, I say, on the LORD.

PSALM 27:13–14

- Have you ever felt so overwhelmed by your circumstances that you thought you couldn't go on? It's easy to lose sight of the bigger picture when we're in the midst of a trial. King David knew something about troubles. He was anointed as king when he was sixteen, but he was not crowned until he was thirty. During many of the intervening years, he was running for his life from King Saul. Yet he still believed that one day God would bring him out of his trouble and fulfill His Word.

- Do you ever wonder if you will see the goodness of the Lord this side of heaven? David said the only thing keeping him going was believing that God would bring him through to the other side. He knew from experience that God would finish what He started in his life.

- Waiting is difficult. We want our answer and we want it now, but God works on His own timetable. Waiting, however, does not have to be wasted time.

We can use the time to prepare ourselves for the task God has assigned us. What are you waiting on? Is there some way you can be preparing for God's answer to arrive?

- David also says we should be of good courage because God is with us and will strengthen us so that we can persevere through the tough times. David refused to kill Saul on several occasions because he said he could not kill God's anointed. It was God's place to remove Saul when He saw fit. The Bible is full of people who rushed to make something happen, only to cause trouble for everyone involved. What are the possible consequences if you try to get ahead of God's plan?

- We can trust God to work things out for the best, because He knows the future and all the possible outcomes, and He has our best interest at heart. So, wait on the Lord and you will see His goodness.

Father, help me have patience to wait for You.
Give me Your strength so that I can have
the courage to persevere. I trust Your
timing, and I will wait on You.

A Rock to Stand On

He is the Rock, his work is perfect: for all his ways are judgment: a God of truth and without iniquity, just and right is he.

DEUTERONOMY 32:4

- Have you ever walked on uneven ground or sand? Doesn't it feel good to step onto solid ground? Life is like that too. When it feels like the very ground under your feet is no longer stable, you can stand on the rock that will not be moved.

- In this chapter of scripture, Moses is showing why God is to be honored, stirring Israel about their wickedness, and justifying God's actions against them. In this verse, he is focusing on the character of God. Because of Christ's death, burial, and resurrection, we are able to claim the position of children of God and all the benefits that go with it. We can rest knowing that we have a firm foundation, regardless of what is going on around us.

- What can we expect from God? He is a rock that is unmovable and immutable, meaning He will never change. Even as the world around you is in constant upheaval, God remains the one you can count on. His work is perfect, meaning that it is complete and lacking nothing, which includes the work of salvation and justification in you. He is a God of truth and will never lie to you. He is without sin, so you can trust that He will never do anything to harm you. Finally, He is just and right, so you can expect fair dealings.

- God is a rock you can stand on in good times and bad. No matter what you do, He will always be there. If you walk away, He will be waiting for you right where you left Him. Even if the world falls apart around you, God is the rock that will not be moved, a safe place for you to run to. Better yet, He is a rock on which we can abide forever.

Father, in a world that is always changing, it's reassuring to know that we have a place to run to that is unchanging. I have a rock I can hold to that is holding on to me. When I stray from Your presence, I know You are always waiting to welcome me home. You are my rock.

Catch Me When I Fall

The eternal God is thy refuge, and underneath are the everlasting arms: and he shall thrust out the enemy from before thee; and shall say, Destroy them.

DEUTERONOMY 33:27

- Have you ever played one of those games where you have to carefully remove one piece without disturbing the rest? One wrong move and the whole thing comes tumbling down around you. With a game, you can reset and play again, but in real life sometimes it feels like we are tight-rope walking without a net and one wrong move can spell disaster. For the Christian, we have something even better than a net.

- What do you trust? In this verse, Moses is singing a song about God as a place of refuge and security. People trust in money, careers, power, noble causes, or even dreams, but these are all temporal things that can change in an instant. Instead, we have an eternal refuge who does not change, if we will only learn to trust Him.

- Have you suffered the loss of a loved one or a job and felt like the floor had fallen out beneath you? God is waiting with outstretched arms to catch you when you fall. He is strong enough, and His strength never weakens. He has everlasting arms that will always be our safe place, where no storm can destroy us.

- Have you ever hesitated to do something that God has called you to do because you are afraid you will fail? Those without God must be forever cautious, because one mistake could mean losing everything. As Christians, we can be bold because even if we do fail, we have a refuge to run to and everlasting arms to catch us when we fall.

- What about those who want you to fail? You also don't have to worry about opposition or enemies. As your refuge, God will protect you even at your most vulnerable moments and win the battle for you.

Father, I'm grateful for Your everlasting arms that wait to catch me when I fall and for a refuge to hide in when things fall apart. I know You will protect me from those who want to see me fail and You will help me begin again. May I be bold in Your name as I go forth in the world and show others Your love and mercy.

Battling the Spirit of Fear

For God hath not given us the spirit of fear;
but of power, and of love, and of a sound mind.

2 TIMOTHY 1:7

- The world can be a scary place, but there is a time and a place for a healthy fear. When fear makes us more cautious about driving on wet roads or dealing with dangerous chemicals, it's a healthy fear. However, when our lives seem to be consumed with fear that keeps us from living our lives, then it has become an unhealthy fear. How do you tell the difference?

- If your fear motivates you to do something such as slow down because of danger signs, then it's healthy. If it freezes you so that you can't take action, then it's a problem. The second kind of fear is from the enemy, but God has given you ways to battle this spirit of fear.

- God has given you power through the Holy Spirit, who lives within you. The Spirit is a source of strength you can plug into at any time and has power to overcome fear. Just His presence can eliminate fear. He has given you the power of protection as well as the power of His promises to you. We can depend upon Him to be our shield and refuge.

- God has given us perfect love, which casts out fear. He has called you and equipped you to do His work. When God starts something, He always finishes, so you don't have to be afraid. God's love is also joyful, and joy can dispel fear. When fear tries to rear its ugly head, pray, read the Bible, call a friend, or just do an activity that brings you joy.

- God's Word can give you a sound mind. Focus on the truth of His Word and the fact that He is with you no matter what. He is the one who is in control, and you can rest knowing that He only wants your best.

- What are you afraid of? God has given you ways to battle the spirit of fear. Don't let fear keep you from doing what God has called you to do.

Father, thank You for the weapons You have given me to battle the spirit of fear. Help me to keep moving forward no matter what is going on in the world, because I can rest in Your presence and power.

The God Who Sees Me

*And he said, Hagar, Sarai's maid, whence camest thou?
and whither wilt thou go? And she said, I flee from the
face of my mistress Sarai. . . . And she called the name of
the Lord that spake unto her, Thou God seest me: for she
said, Have I also here looked after him that seeth me?*

GENESIS 16:8, 13

- Have you ever felt invisible, like no one sees the
  real you? Hagar was Sarah's handmaid. Sarah
  decided that she would give Hagar to her husband,
  Abraham, so that she could give them an heir. When
  Hagar became pregnant, the trouble started, so
  Hagar ran away because no one would take her
  side. Have you ever felt caught in a situation that
  wasn't of your making?

- As she was running away, God asked her a couple
  of questions. Sometimes in order to understand
  our current situation, we need to see how we got
  there: Where have you come from? How did you
  get here? If you ask God, He will show you.

- Where are you going? Hagar really didn't know,
  and sometimes neither do we. God often uses
  questions to help us see truth in our lives. God is
  always waiting for us with open arms. All we have
  to do is ask Him. Hagar realized she had no place

to go and no plan. She knew she needed God's help. He told her to go back to her mistress and that He would bless her and her son.

- Hagar called God by a name that means "the God who sees me." Even when no one else sees you, God does. He knows your situation and is waiting to guide you if you turn to Him. Where have you come from? Where are you going? God is listening and waiting for your answer. He wants to guide you through the lonely and difficult times as much as He does through the good times. He is faithful no matter what.

Father, sometimes I feel invisible, like no one sees me, but I know You are the God who sees. You see each and every one of Your children and are interested in their daily lives. I know You see me even in my darkest hours. I long for Your presence and guidance as I try to find my way forward through the darkness.

Work of Art

*For we are his workmanship, created in Christ
Jesus unto good works, which God hath before
ordained that we should walk in them.*

EPHESIANS 2:10

- Have you ever been to an art museum or exhibit and
  looked at the art? There are all kinds of art forms
  and styles in all the colors of the rainbow. The world
  is God's art museum. He paints beautiful sunrises
  and sunsets, fields of flowers, and forests full of
  stately trees. His favorite work of art, though, is us.

- Do you feel unimportant? We are His workmanship,
  and we are important to God. He created us and
  gave us free will so that we could have a relationship
  with Him. We are His treasures and the apple of
  His eye. No one will ever love us more than He does.

- Do you ever feel useless? Remember that God
  has a purpose for each of His children, including you. Even before you were born, God knew who
  you would be and what you would do. He created
  you so that you could do good works. God wants
  a relationship with us, but He also wants us to
  join Him in His work in the world. The church is
  God's body on the earth, and each of us plays a role
  in that body. What has God gifted you to do?

- Do you ever feel like time has passed you by? It's not too late to join God in the family business. As long as we have breath, God has a purpose and a place for us. We are here to testify about what God has done for us, to lead others to salvation, and to build our community. What task has God given to you?

- While good works won't win us salvation, since it's a gift of God that no one can earn, good works are a way to show our gratitude. They are an overflowing of our love for God that give us purpose and joy.

Father, I'm thankful that You chose me before I was born to be Your work of art. As Your workmanship, I know that I am created to do good works, to join You in the family business of reconciling humankind to You. Show me my place in Your world so that I can do what I was created to do.

On-the-Job Training

All scripture is given by inspiration of God, and is profitable for doctrine, for reproof, for correction, for instruction in righteousness: that the man of God may be perfect, thoroughly furnished unto all good works.

2 TIMOTHY 3:16–17

- Have you ever started a new job that offered on-the-job training, only it wasn't very helpful? You still felt lost and unequipped to do the tasks that were asked of you. Did you wish for a training manual that showed you what to do? The Christian life has both a training manual and on-the-job training available to everyone.

- The Bible is our training manual. It's useful for doctrine, which gives us the truths we need to know. It's also good for reproof, which lets us know where we need work or improvement. Correction lets us know what we're doing wrong so that we can correct it. Instruction gives us the direction we should take.

- How do you use the training manual? First, you read it, but reading it won't make you a better Christian unless you apply what you have learned. This is where on-the-job training comes into play. As you seek to apply the Bible to your everyday life, the

Holy Spirit will show you what you're doing right and what needs work.

- What if you need more help? God has assigned more seasoned Christians as supervisors and trainers to help you along, such as pastors, Bible study leaders, and mature Christians. They can help you along like good coworkers in Christ. However, everything is subject to the Bible. It's wise to check someone else's leading against the Word of God. We are commanded to verify everything we believe in light of the scriptures. So, don't be afraid to question. God is not afraid of questions, and church leaders shouldn't be either.

Father, I thank You that You inspired the Bible so that I could have Your teaching for how to live the Christian life and be in a right relationship with You. I'm grateful that You train and equip us to do what You have called us to do. I ask the Holy Spirit's help in rightly divining the scriptures and discerning false teaching. Show me how to apply the scriptures every day as I seek to do Your will.

Overcomer

Ye are of God, little children, and have
overcome them: because greater is he that
is in you, than he that is in the world.

1 JOHN 4:4

- Do you like a movie about someone overcoming great obstacles to pursue a dream? You hold your breath as you watch them fall down and then get back up. You cheer them on as they struggle to the finish line, and you celebrate as they finally reach their goal. What is it about these stories that tugs at our hearts? Maybe it's because we all struggle sometimes, and we find inspiration in seeing someone actually overcome great obstacles to reach a goal.

- What are you struggling against? John was writing to warn Christians about antichrists and false teachers of their day. We too are surrounded by false teachings, sometimes even within the church. John assures the church that they have the divine power within them that is greater than these fatal delusions of the day. We are God's children, and we have the Holy Spirit within us to help us discern truth from lies.

- Who is winning? The scripture gives us hope for victory. You have already overcome the obstacles you are facing, because you have overcome obstacles in the past. How has God helped you in the past? He has not changed. He is still overcoming obstacles, and He will keep you from being led astray if you only ask.

- The world is easily led astray and carried away by every wind of false doctrine. They are easily changed, but you have a firm foundation and will not be moved from your beliefs because of the Holy Spirit within you and your relationship with Christ that is built on trust and a history of reliability.

- As you face obstacles, remember that you can overcome whatever you face because Christ has already overcome the world. Take your burdens to Him, and He will do battle for you. He is greater than any power in the world, and that is something you can count on.

Father, I'm thankful that Jesus has already overcome the world. Through His sacrifice on the cross and His resurrection, I now have the gift of salvation and the Holy Spirit within me so that I can overcome every challenge. You are greater than anything I will ever face, so I have hope for victory because Christ lives.

A New You

Therefore if any man be in Christ, he is a new creature: old things are passed away; behold, all things are become new.

2 CORINTHIANS 5:17

- Have you ever watched a makeover show? Whether it's a person's look and wardrobe or a house renovation, we all love to see the before and after photographs. We are often amazed by the difference. You might even wish you could get a free makeover. If you are a Christian, you have already gotten a spiritual makeover.

- Do you ever struggle in your Christian walk? We all do. However, we all were given a makeover when we accepted Christ as Lord.

- How does that work? It's kind of like a home renovation. It doesn't matter what our lives were like before Christ because He is a master carpenter. He strips everything down to the studs and removes all the sin. Then, the Holy Spirit moves in and begins work to turn us into a suitable home for God. The old things have been removed, and all new fittings and furnishings have been installed.

- What about the outside? When God works on the inside, it should show on the outside like the glow of a new coat of paint from the light spilling out from the windows. This side of heaven, our "house" will be subject to the elements and always in need of repair, but it will never be the old house again.

- When God does a makeover, it's permanent. The old has been demolished and replaced by the new. You can't go back, but would you ever want to? Sometimes we get tired of the sound of renovation in our souls, but the end result is worth it. When we reach heaven, the final reveal will be a new body and spirit that are perfect and eternal.

Father, I am a new creature. When the enemy tries to tell me that I'm a failure, I can point to the day of my salvation and know I was truly changed. I know I'm still a work in progress, but You are faithful to complete what You have started in me. I have the hope of an eternal body one day, but in the meantime I'm thankful You have changed me forever.

Fresh Start

*If we confess our sins, he is faithful and
just to forgive us our sins, and to cleanse
us from all unrighteousness.*

1 JOHN 1:9

- Do you ever want a do-over? In golf it's called a
  mulligan when a shot is not counted during an
  unofficial game. Sometimes we want to take
  back something we said, get a second chance at
  a relationship, or just redo a task at work minus
  a mistake. The world often doesn't allow for a do-
  over, but God is the God of second chances.

- Throughout the Bible, we read about people who
  made mistakes and failed God. King David, a man
  after God's own heart, committed adultery and
  murder, yet God still used him mightily. Jonah
  refused to take God's message to Nineveh and spent
  three days in the belly of a whale, but God still
  used him to deliver His message. What made the
  difference? God's only requirement for a do-over
  is to confess our sins and repent.

- Have you ever admitted to doing something but
  tried to gloss it over with excuses or explanations?
  How does it make you feel when someone does that
  to you? When someone does something wrong, we

want them to admit what they have done and admit that it was wrong. Then, we have to repent, which means turn away from that behavior in the future. In order to receive forgiveness, we have to be sorry we sinned and not just sorry we got caught. God is faithful to forgive if we are sincere.

• Have you ever had someone say they forgive you and then later bring up past wrongs? God does not do that. When He forgives you, He forgets it as if it never happened. He wipes the slate clean so that it's gone forever. If you hear a voice reminding you of your past sins and you have confessed them to God, then that is the voice of the enemy trying to steal your peace and your joy. Silence that voice and claim God's promise of forgiveness.

Father, I'm grateful for Your mercy and grace that offers forgiveness when I fail. You give me a true do-over because You forgive and forget, wiping the slate clean so that I can have a fresh start. You throw it away as far as the east is from the west, never to be brought up again or to weigh on my future. Praise be to God!

From Where I Stand

Therefore being justified by faith, we have peace with God through our Lord Jesus Christ: by whom also we have access by faith into this grace wherein we stand, and rejoice in hope of the glory of God.

ROMANS 5:1–2

- We all have opinions on a variety of topics. Have you ever heard someone say, "From where I stand..."? They usually go on to explain their opinion based on their perspective of the issue. Conservationists are worried about trees, and lumber mills are worried about their livelihood. The key to winning a debate is to have a firm foundation from which to argue your point. Do you struggle to find peace? Then you need to know where you stand with God.

- We are justified by faith, and faith helps us realize we are delivered from our past by Christ's death. Because of what He did, we have salvation that is not based on our works. No one can ever say that we don't deserve forgiveness because of our past or that we are not good enough.

- Because of Christ, we also have access to grace and are privileged to be declared not guilty. Even more, we are children of God, along with all the benefits that brings. We are joint heirs with Christ to all that belongs to God. Because of Christ, we also have hope of a future here on earth and an eternity in heaven with Him. Because of Christ, God's love fills our lives and gives us the ability to reach out to others.

- Where do you stand? As a Christian, you stand in grace where there is faith, hope, and love. There is also peace. It's all available because of the grace of God. Our perspective should always come from our position in Christ, which is not subject to the world's rules. When the enemy tries to rattle you and take your peace, remember the grace wherein you stand and hold firm. The world has no authority over a child of the King.

Father, I'm grateful for Your grace because the benefits are limitless. I have faith, hope, love, peace, and access to Your throne to petition for my needs. You give me strength and purpose. You give me hope for a future in heaven. From where I stand, Christ is all I need, and I stand firm in the gift of God's grace.

Whose We Are

But now thus saith the LORD that created thee,
O Jacob, and he that formed thee, O Israel, Fear not:
for I have redeemed thee, I have called thee by thy
name; thou art mine. When thou passest through the
waters, I will be with thee; and through the rivers,
they shall not overflow thee: when thou walkest
through the fire, thou shalt not be burned; neither
shall the flame kindle upon thee. For I am the LORD
thy God, the Holy One of Israel, thy Saviour: I gave
Egypt for thy ransom, Ethiopia and Seba for thee.

ISAIAH 43:1–3

- Are you afraid? The world is full of darkness and danger, but we don't have to be afraid because of whose we are. We are children of the Lord God, who is holy and powerful. When you feel fear come creeping in, take a moment to remember who is in control.

- Are you worried about eternity? God is our Creator, and He is also our Redeemer. When we accepted Christ, we became His and were put under His protection. We are called by His name, so the enemy can no longer touch us. Our eternity is secure.

- Are you treading water in your finances and relationships? God is with you when you go through the water. He never said life would be perfect, but He did say He would get you safely to the other side.

- Are you going through the fire of trials and tribulations? God is with you just like He was with the three Hebrew children in the Old Testament. We cannot expect to escape troubles in this life, but God will lead us to the other side. Even if it means death, we will still pass through in His hands safely to eternity.

- No matter what you are going through, you don't have to be afraid because God is with you, and He is in control of circumstances. We can trust Him to get us through whatever comes our way.

Father, I'm thankful for whose I am. You are the Most High God, and You have called me and redeemed me and given me Your name. I don't have to be afraid of anything in this world. Your presence goes with me, and Your wings of protection are around me even if I can't sense You in the moment.

Promise Keeper

For all the promises of God in him are yea, and in him Amen, unto the glory of God by us. Now he which stablisheth us with you in Christ, and hath anointed us, is God; who hath also sealed us, and given the earnest of the Spirit in our hearts.

2 Corinthians 1:20–22

- Has anyone ever broken a promise to you? In this world, that is an all-too-common issue. It's hard to find someone who keeps their promises, whether it's following through on something as big as wedding vows or as small as picking up a loaf of bread. There is one we can count on who always keeps His promises.

- The Bible is full of promises, all of which God will keep. If He said He would do it, He will. Now, some of those promises come with conditions, but He is faithful to do His part when we do our part. For example, salvation requires us to repent of our sins and confess Jesus as Lord. When we do that, we have the gift of salvation and eternity in heaven with Him. Are you waiting on God to fulfill a promise? Are you keeping your side of the deal?

- God is the one who anointed us, so if He approves, no other can condemn us. Is the enemy telling you not to believe in God's promises? Does he tell you that you aren't worthy? God's promises are based not on our worthiness but on His grace, which is based on Christ's works. We can trust God to do what He says.

- Does the enemy sometimes make you doubt your salvation? If you have truly given your heart to Christ, then God has also given you the Holy Spirit as proof of ownership. Because we have the Holy Spirit, we have the peace of God and hope of eternity to come.

Father, I'm thankful that You keep Your promises even when no one else does. I can count on You to follow through. Not one of Your promises will fail. I thank You for the presence of the Holy Spirit in my life so that I have proof that I am one of Yours and that a home in heaven with You awaits every believer, including me. You are a promise keeper, so I have nothing to fear.

Out of the Darkness

Who hath delivered us from the power of darkness,
and hath translated us into the kingdom of his dear Son.

COLOSSIANS 1:13

- Why is a power outage in a storm so disturbing? Is it the suddenness? Is it the feeling of isolation and lack of communication? Is it the inability to see clearly? Darkness brings fear unless you have a source of light.

- When the power goes out, a small flashlight can bring a sense of relief and peace, even though your situation has not changed. When we were lost in sin, darkness had power over us because we didn't have access to the light. When Christ came into our hearts, He brought light to us. It came to our lives in the form of the Holy Spirit. No matter what darkness there may be in the world, we always have access to the light.

- Now that we have the light, it's up to us to share it with others who are sitting in the darkness. It doesn't take much light to dispel darkness. Think of a night-light in a child's bedroom. The tiny light brings peace and comfort to a sleeping child. How much more can the light of Christ make a difference in a dark world?

- We don't have to run from the darkness anymore. It has no power over us unless we let it. So, when the darkness seems to overtake your world, let the light of Christ dispel the darkness. If we join with other Christians, imagine how much of a difference we could make in this world.

- The enemy will try to make you afraid to share your light. He will tell you people won't like it or will think you're weird. He will find all kinds of reasons for you to keep the light to yourself because he knows that light will always beat darkness. Who needs your light to shine in their lives?

Father, I'm thankful that the light of Your Son is shining in me so that darkness no longer has power over me. When I go into the dark world, help me have courage to shine the light of Your love and to help others to step into Your light.

Free Indeed

*If the Son therefore shall make you free,
ye shall be free indeed.*

JOHN 8:36

- What does it mean to be free? For some people,
  freedom is being able to do whatever they like
  whenever they like, regardless of who it affects.
  They say it's their right to be free, but who gave
  them that right? What did it cost?

- Have you heard the saying that freedom isn't
  free? Most people are referring to the members
  of the military who fought and died to defend our
  freedoms, but the true source of freedom is not
  because of anything any human has ever done. No
  matter how hard we try, we cannot free ourselves
  from sin or its consequences. It took Christ's death,
  burial, and resurrection to free us from sin and
  death, so when He makes you free, you are truly
  free.

- What does freedom look like? Some people think
  freedom is being able to do anything you want.
  What they don't see is that sin enslaves you. So
  many sins may seem enjoyable for a season, but
  eventually they can take over your life. You no
  longer have control; sin does. Giving our lives to

Christ's control frees us to be the people we were meant to be.

- We also have freedom of the mind because the truth of Christ empowers us to see beyond ourselves and see the bigger picture of eternity. No longer are we bound by earthly wisdom, which is limited and selfish because it is bound by lusts and passion. When we submit in obedience to Christ, we are submitting to a God who loves us and wants our best. He wants to give us the gift of eternity in heaven with Him in a perfect body that is eternally free.

- What is trying to hold you hostage? Give it to Christ, because He is the only one who can truly free you. It probably won't be easy. It will probably be a daily struggle. However, the end result is worth the effort and pain. The only true freedom is in following Christ with our whole heart.

Father, I thank You that the Son has made me free from sin and its dominion. When I'm tempted, please make a way for me to escape temptation's grip. Help me live in obedience to You so that I can be truly free.

Perfect Love

Herein is our love made perfect, that we may have
boldness in the day of judgment: because as he is,
so are we in this world. There is no fear in love;
but perfect love casteth out fear: because fear
hath torment. He that feareth is not made perfect
in love. We love him, because he first loved us.

1 JOHN 4:17–19

- Are you feeling overwhelmed by the worries of the world? Sometimes it's beyond overwhelming when everything seems to be falling down around you. Yet, there is a truth we can depend on in times like these: God is love. Because He loves us, He will make a way for us. It may not be exactly as we planned, but in the end it will be for our benefit and the glory of God.

- Have you ever tried to make someone love you? It doesn't work, because love is a choice. God chose to love us, and He is the source of love. Our love is a response to God's love and not the basis of His love for us. He loved us when we were unlovable. He loved us when we took no thought of Him. He loves us no matter what we do. However, that doesn't mean there aren't consequences for our actions when we sin against Him. It does mean that we can repent and return to Him time and again, and He will restore us to a right relationship out of His love for us.

- How do we respond to God's love? Love one another. John doesn't tell us that because God loves us, we ought to love Him. That is a given, but if we love God, then it should work itself out by loving those who need love. The lost without Christ haven't received His love yet, so love for God will manifest itself by self-sacrificing love for others. They, the world, will know us by our love.

- What is perfect love? The word *perfect* in scripture actually means "complete." Because of God's love, we don't have to be afraid. We can go boldly to the throne on the day of judgment knowing that we have been adopted as one of His children. We can trust in His love with full confidence.

Father, I love You. Thank You for Your perfect love that casts out fear. Help me to show love to those around me who need Your love.

Inseparable

Who shall separate us from the love of Christ? shall tribulation, or distress, or persecution, or famine, or nakedness, or peril, or sword? As it is written, For thy sake we are killed all the day long; we are accounted as sheep for the slaughter. Nay, in all these things we are more than conquerors through him that loved us. For I am persuaded, that neither death, nor life, nor angels, nor principalities, nor powers, nor things present, nor things to come, nor height, nor depth, nor any other creature, shall be able to separate us from the love of God, which is in Christ Jesus our Lord.

ROMANS 8:35–39

- Did you ever have a friend you spent so much time with that people said you were inseparable? While we may spend a lot of time with certain people, it's almost impossible to be inseparable. We will spend some time apart even from spouses, even if only an hour or two. There is only one that we can say is inseparable, and that is God. No matter where we go, God is with us.

- What can separate us from the love of Christ? The short answer is nothing, but Paul goes into greater detail to make it clear. First, he lists events that could separate people, like tribulation, famine, or war, but he says we are more than conquerors of these things because of Christ. Then he lists a series of potential things that might separate people and concludes that none of it can separate us from God's love. Neither fear of death nor the pleasures of life, neither the good nor the bad angels, neither present troubles nor those to come, no matter how high or low we go in society, nothing can separate us from the love of God.

- We are more than conquerors over all these things because Christ has already won the victory over each of them. So, we need not fear, for God's love will help us endure and overcome them.

Father, no trial, famine, war, or even death can separate me from Your love. I'm thankful that the work of Christ has overcome all things so that I can endure anything through Your strength. Your presence is always with me no matter what happens in this world. You and I are truly inseparable.

Peculiar People

But ye are a chosen generation, a royal priesthood,
an holy nation, a peculiar people; that ye should
shew forth the praises of him who hath called
you out of darkness into his marvellous light.

1 PETER 2:9

- What do you think of when you hear the word *peculiar*? Most people think of words like *strange*, *weird*, or *odd*, but those aren't the only meanings. Do people think you are odd or peculiar? Take it as a compliment because it also means "uncommon," "unusual," or "distinctive." It also means "belonging characteristically to something"—in our case, to Christ. So, how are we like Him?

- We are a chosen generation. God picked us to be on His team. God offers everyone a chance to join Him, but only a few choose to respond to the call. How does it feel to be chosen by the almighty God?

- We are a royal priesthood. When Christ died on the cross and was resurrected, the final sacrifice was made. Animal sacrifice and a complicated system are no longer necessary. We have access directly to God and can join Him in His work. How great is that?

- We are a holy nation because we are called to a higher standard than the world. We show love to one another and promote peace. We act with justice and speak the truth. Are you trying to live up to God's standard? We will never be perfect, but we should strive each day to be more like Jesus.

- We are a peculiar people because of Christ's work on the cross and the Holy Spirit within us. We have taken on the characteristics of Christ so that we are peculiar to Him. We are called out of darkness into His light so that we can be a light to a lost world. Given all that, who wouldn't want to be peculiar?

Father, I admit that sometimes I really want to fit in, but most of the time I'm happy to be peculiar, especially in our world today. There is joy in being chosen by You and living a life set apart. I'm grateful that I can go directly to Your throne in boldness with Christ as my only mediator. I want to be such an example of Christ that others long to be peculiar too. Help me shine Your light today.

Looking for a Home

For our conversation is in heaven;
from whence also we look for the
Saviour, the Lord Jesus Christ.

PHILIPPIANS 3:20

- Are you looking for a home, some place to belong? Even the home and family we have known all our lives can fall apart or be separated. Sometimes we can lose our physical home to financial problems, fire, or storms. We all want a safe place to land and feel secure. However, as Christians we are sojourners on earth, so we will never feel truly at home this side of heaven.

- Do you feel at odds in society? In this passage, the word *conversation* can also be translated "citizenship." Our citizenship is in heaven, so our time on earth is like having a work visa in a foreign country. We are in a culture that is strange to us, in which we should never feel truly at ease. We speak the language of light and love in a world that is full of darkness.

- Do you have family that is far off? We can't wait until times like the holidays when we can be together. Heaven is the same. We have loved ones who have already gone to heaven, but our Father and our Savior are there too. Can you imagine what it will be like to actually be face-to-face with Jesus?

- Don't worry if you never feel like you fit in here. You were never meant to belong here. God has a better place for us, but in the meantime He has work for us to do, bringing as many as we can out of the darkness and into His light. Keep your focus on Jesus, and the things of this world will lose their importance. Is there someone you want to invite to your heavenly home?

Father, the earth is not my home, but sometimes I forget that as I try so hard to fit in with the crowd. Then I remember that heaven is my real home where my place is secure. In the meantime, help me keep my focus on You and Your purpose for my life so that I can take as many people home to heaven with me as possible. There is always room for one more at Your table.

You Get Me

O lord, thou hast searched me, and known me. Thou knowest my downsitting and mine uprising, thou understandest my thought afar off. Thou compassest my path and my lying down, and art acquainted with all my ways.

PSALM 139:1–3

- Have you ever met someone you just seemed to click with? Maybe it was a best friend or a romantic interest. They just seemed to "get you." They knew you, understood you, and still loved you. The truth is, while we may have close relationships, we never truly know everything about someone—or even ourselves for that matter. But there is one who gets everything about us.

- Who knows you better than anyone? God does. He has searched us even down to the darkest corners of our hearts, where all our secrets lie. We don't even know all the darkness in our hearts, but God does and still loves us.

- Our Father knows when we go to bed and when we get up and everything we do in between. Nothing is hidden from Him, not even the things we do in the dark, yet He still loves us.

- Have you ever finished someone else's thought, and that person said, "You read my mind"? God can do even more than read your mind. He hears your thoughts no matter how far away you might try to get.

- Does anyone know you like God? No. He is acquainted with everything about you because He surrounds you with His presence. He knows what you like and what you don't like. He really gets you, and He really loves you.

- Have you ever thought that if someone truly knew you, they wouldn't love you? There is one who knows you, gets you, and loves you no matter what you say or do. What could be better than that?

Father, I know You get me even when others don't. You see me, You hear me, You know me, and You love me. You are always with me, and for that I am forever grateful. Help me to love others as You love me, even when it's difficult, so that they can find their way to You.

Marvelous Work

*For thou hast possessed my reins: thou hast covered
me in my mother's womb. I will praise thee; for I am
fearfully and wonderfully made: marvellous are
thy works; and that my soul knoweth right well.*

PSALM 139:13–14

- Has someone ever looked at your work and said you did a good job? It's amazing what a little word of praise can do to lift our spirits and boost our confidence. Are you feeling a little low on confidence? Do you need a little spiritual boost? Then consider that you are one of God's most marvelous works.

- When you look at yourself in the mirror, what do you see? God sees His creation, a work of art. He is the one who holds the reins, so He is the one in charge. When we commit ourselves to Christ, He takes possession. But even before that, He was our Creator who knew every detail about us. God doesn't make mistakes, so His artwork is just as He planned.

- Who do you look like? Parents often discuss who their child resembles in the family, but spiritually speaking, we take after our Father. We are fearfully and wonderfully made because we are made in His image. God's character goes into your creation, so when you feel worthless, remember who you resemble. We should have the same respect for ourselves that God has for us. You have to love yourself in order to love others.

- Is there anyone you can't love? We must remember that every human being was created in the image of God, and God loves them. Sometimes it's difficult to love some people, but if we look hard enough, we can see God's mark within them. We can love them, even when they are not lovable, because God loved us even when we were in sin.

- Now look in the mirror and what do you see? God sees His work and thinks it's marvelous. Who are you to argue with God?

Father, You are my Creator, and I am fearfully and wonderfully made in Your image. Help me to see what You see in me, and then help me to see that in others. We all resemble our Father, but sometimes we need a little reminder of what that means. I want to look more like You every day.

Blessed beyond Measure

Blessed be the God and Father of our Lord Jesus Christ, who hath blessed us with all spiritual blessings in heavenly places in Christ.

EPHESIANS 1:3

- Have you ever sat around feeling sorry for yourself and your lot in life? You look at other people, and they seem to have it so much easier than you or have so much more than you. It's a human condition to look at what we don't have when we should be looking at what we do have. Just think about the garden of Eden. Adam and Eve were in paradise, but all they noticed was the one thing they didn't have. So, what is the cure?

- What do you have? The main cure is just to take stock of what you do have. You have salvation and a secure place in eternity with God. That alone is everything to be grateful for, but God is a gracious giver, and He gives us so much more. As the Father of Jesus, our mediator, we now have Him as our heavenly Father who is the giver of all spiritual blessings.

- What are spiritual blessings? First, of course, is salvation, but there are many others, such as gifts of the Spirit and the fruits of the Spirit. We have the presence of the Holy Spirit in our lives every day. We have life and the power to do God's will. We have hope of eternity with Christ. Count your blessings because they are many.

- Now that you have started counting, what can you do? Praise God because He is the one who gives us these blessings, and He is the only one who can. When you started listing your blessings, did you find your heart was lighter? Did your list keep growing? We have blessings beyond measure to be thankful for, so whenever you are feeling down about your circumstances, put your focus on what you do have. Start counting your blessings, and feel your spirit start to rise in gratitude.

Father, all that we have, all that we are, and all that we will be comes from You. I am blessed beyond measure, even though I sometimes forget. As I count my many blessings, I see what amazing gifts You have given me, and I praise Your name for them all.

Branches and the Vine

*Abide in me, and I in you. As the branch cannot bear
fruit of itself, except it abide in the vine; no more can
ye, except ye abide in me. I am the vine, ye are the
branches: He that abideth in me, and I in him, the
same bringeth forth much fruit: for without me ye can
do nothing. If a man abide not in me, he is cast forth
as a branch, and is withered; and men gather them,
and cast them into the fire, and they are burned. If
ye abide in me, and my words abide in you, ye shall
ask what ye will, and it shall be done unto you.*

JOHN 15:4–7

- When pruning a plant, a gardener notices which
  branches are dead and which ones are still full of
  life. Spiritually speaking, what kind of branch are
  you: dead or full of life?

- How do you tell if a branch is alive? It will bear
  fruit. In order to bear fruit, the branch must be
  connected to the vine, where nutrients are found.
  Jesus is the vine, and when we accepted Him as
  Lord, we were grafted onto the vine so that we
  could abide in Him and He in us.

- What does it mean to abide? It means living together
  in unity and proximity. To abide means we move in
  with Christ to live day by day. He doesn't just have

visitation rights; He is our full-time guardian. If you don't maintain the relationship, your branch withers and is useless.

- What are the benefits of abiding? Besides the fact that you won't be pruned, there is the added benefit of answered prayer. To abide means you are in agreement with Him and His will, so anything you ask will be granted because you already agree. Who wouldn't want to abide?

- There is also the benefit of playing a role in bearing fruit. When we are connected to the vine, we become a conduit so that God can work through us to achieve His purposes. There is joy in working with God that cannot be measured.

- So, what kind of branch are you? What kind do you want to be?

Father, I want to be a fruit-filled branch full of Your life and power. I want to see the fruit of Your labor. I want to be a conduit of Your power and join You in the work You have for me to do.

Ask for Directions

Trust in the Lord with all thine heart; and lean not unto thine own understanding. In all thy ways acknowledge him, and he shall direct thy paths.

Proverbs 3:5–6

- Have you ever had to stop for directions? How long did you drive around before you finally asked someone? Even in today's world of GPS and step-by-step instructions on our smartphones or in our cars, we can still get off track or confused. Sometimes landmarks have changed or roads have been rerouted, and the software hasn't been updated. And electronics have meltdowns too. Whatever the reason, sometimes you need a reliable guide who has been there before.

- Who do you trust? We often say we trust God, but do we really trust Him with everything we have, with our whole heart? We often pray for things we need and then set about figuring how to get them ourselves. That is the equivalent to putting an address in the GPS and then looking for a different route. Trusting God means leaning on His guidance and not our own understanding.

- What is wrong with our own understanding? It's faulty. God knows more than we do, whether we like to admit it or not. Expert opinions are valuable, but there is no greater expert than God. He is the Creator after all. He is also perfect and without flaw, so He doesn't make mistakes. No one else can say that.

- How do you acknowledge Him? If you come humbly before Him and admit that you don't know everything and ask for His help, He will give you good directions. Sometimes He takes us on the scenic route, but it's always for our good.

- When do you ask for directions? It's best to ask directions before we start so that we can get off on the right foot, but God will still help us when we are lost in the woods. We just have to pull over and ask for directions.

Father, when I lose my way, I'm so glad that You are ready and willing to help me get back on the right path, in the right direction. Help me put aside my pride. I humbly ask You to direct my life day to day. Help me to trust that You know better and will never lead me astray.

Strength to Climb

*The LORD God is my strength, and he will make
my feet like hinds' feet, and he will make me
to walk upon mine high places. To the chief
singer on my stringed instruments.*

HABAKKUK 3:19

- Do you ever feel like you're surrounded by chaos
  and confusion? Does it feel like you're down in a
  pit and can't see your way out? Too often we try to
  rely on our own strength to get out of situations or
  to do a task, but it's only through God's strength
  that we are able to do anything.

- Have you ever been in a situation and wondered
  how you were going to get out of it? Habakkuk
  could relate. God had shown him that sad times
  were coming to His people, but his feelings were
  not controlled by the situation. He was trusting
  by faith in God's ability to give him strength to get
  through the coming storm. When nothing makes
  sense and troubles seem beyond what you can
  handle, remember that God gives strength. It is not
  human strength; it is His supernatural strength.
  That is how we can endure all things.

- What mountain do you need to climb? Whose
  strength are you using to climb? God-sized

mountains require God-sized strength. He is waiting for you to ask, and He will give you what you need for the task ahead. He will strengthen your faith and take you to the high places. All you have to do is ask for the strength to climb.

Father, I see a mountain ahead that I don't think I can climb, at least not in my own strength. Please give me Your strength so that I can walk on the high places with You.

The Lord's Delight

Delight thyself also in the LORD: and he shall give thee the desires of thine heart. Commit thy way unto the LORD; trust also in him; and he shall bring it to pass.

PSALM 37:4–5

- How often have you heard people say that God will give you the desires of your heart if you just ask? Have you ever asked for something and gotten a resounding no? Why is that? The problem is that this verse has two parts, and people often overlook the first half. This promise is a conditional one, which means you have to meet the first part to receive the blessing.

- How do you delight yourself in the Lord? Delighting in the Lord is not just about being happy about the gifts He gives. It goes much deeper. We must make God our heart's delight. Our focus must be on Him and His will for us so that we want to please Him. If you find your joy in God and strive to please Him, then He will give you the desires of your heart because your will is lined up with His.

- What does it mean to "commit thy way"? This promise has a two-part provision. If you are obedient to God's commands and follow His leadership and if you trust Him, He will bring it to pass. But what shall He bring to pass? His will in our lives, which may not necessarily be what we requested, but if we are in tune with His will, it will delight us.

- What does it mean to trust Him? A pastor used to give the example of a chair. You can talk about how you trust that the chair will hold your weight all day, but until you actually sit in it, you cannot say that you trust it. If we say that we trust God, we have to let go of our situation and allow Him to work it out as He sees fit. It sounds a little scary until we remember that we're handing it over to God, who doesn't make mistakes and only wants the best for us.

Father, teach me how to delight in You. I want my life to focus on pleasing You so that I can be in Your will. Help me to trust. It's hard for me to relinquish control, but the reality is I don't control the situation. Only You can bring it to pass.

All the Things

*Not that I speak in respect of want: for I have
learned, in whatsoever state I am, therewith to
be content. I know both how to be abased, and I
know how to abound: every where and in all things
I am instructed both to be full and to be hungry,
both to abound and to suffer need. I can do all
things through Christ which strengtheneth me.*

PHILIPPIANS 4:11–13

- Are you tired of trying to do all the things that
  people say you should do? Are you tired of trying
  to have what everyone says you need to have?
  Social media and marketing are constantly trying
  to tell us what will make us happy, but as soon as
  we get the one thing, then there is another new
  thing. The old thing loses its shine as you move
  on to the next. What if there was a different way?

- Are you content? Another word for *contentment* is
  satisfaction. Are you satisfied with what you have
  and where you are? Why or why not? Paul says he
  learned to be content in whatever state he was in. It
  didn't matter if he was rich or poor, full or hungry.
  If God was with him, then he was satisfied because
  God was all he needed.

- Can you do all things? Many people pull out the last verse and try to apply it to whatever it is they want to do, but can you really do all things? No one but God can do all things. Sure, we may try a lot of things, but we also fail at them. When we look at this verse in the context of the other verses, we see that Paul means enduring. He can endure anything because God will give him strength. So, no matter what situation he finds himself in, he knows he can get through it because God will help him through.

- Can you do and have all things? No. Instead of striving to please others or reaching for material things to satisfy, try the things of God. His way is simpler. It's not always easier, but He goes with us and strengthens us. His ways give more satisfaction and contentment than can be found in all the treasures of the world.

Father, I'm tired of doing all the things and striving to attain things that don't satisfy. Help me to learn to be content with whatever You have given me. I know that with Your strength I can endure anything. I want my contentment to be in You.

Fearless

He shall not be afraid of evil tidings:
his heart is fixed, trusting in the LORD.

PSALM 112:7

- Have you ever gotten a phone call that shattered your world? Maybe a loved one was in a car wreck or you suffered a job loss or learned of a serious medical issue. Suddenly your whole world is upside down. What is your response? Do you go to worst-case scenario, or do you go into denial? Either extreme has its pitfalls. This scripture offers us a much better way.

- Where is your focus? When you get the bad news, what is your first thought? If the first thing you do is start listing all the possible negative outcomes, then shift your focus back to Christ. When your focus is on Him, you can gain perspective of the situation. Many times we overreact before anything has even come to pass, causing unnecessary stress. Take a deep breath and pray first. We are to take everything to God in prayer, and He will give us peace.

- Who do you trust? Besides focusing on the Lord, we also need to trust Him to handle the situation. Most of the time, the circumstances are out of our control. We might be able to do a few things, but the final outcome is not within our grasp. When we trust God completely, we find that our fears will subside, even fears of death.

- How do you stop being afraid of evil tidings? First, you have to keep your focus on God and maintain a close relationship. The closer you are to Him, the better your perspective. The enemy wants to send you in a downward spiral of fear and despair. God wants to give you peace and assurance of His presence. Next, work on your trust issues. As we build trust and faith in God, the enemy cannot so easily shake us. We can become fearless when we stand close to God in faith and trust.

Father, in this world I feel like evil tidings are always just around the corner, but You have given us the power over that fear through faith and trust in You. When I remember that You are in control, it takes the burden off me—a burden I can't carry. Thank You for Your grace and mercy. I know I can trust You even to death.

Conspiracy Theories

For the LORD spake thus to me with a strong
hand, and instructed me that I should not walk
in the way of this people, saying, Say ye not,
A confederacy, to all them to whom this people
shall say, A confederacy; neither fear ye their fear,
nor be afraid. Sanctify the LORD of hosts himself;
and let him be your fear, and let him be your dread.

ISAIAH 8:11–13

- Heard any conspiracy theories lately? There are theories about life on other planets, who killed Kennedy, and political intrigue of all kinds. If they were just theories people threw around, they would be harmless, but people become obsessed. Sometimes they become paranoid and afraid, seeking ways to protect themselves from imagined potential danger. While some of the theories might have truth in them, it's the reaction that's the problem.

- Who do you walk with? God commanded Isaiah not to walk in the way of a group of people because of their behavior. Walking with implies that you not only spend a lot of time with someone but also do the things they do. These people were spouting conspiracy theories, and God told Isaiah not to be a part of it because they were spreading fear.

- Who are you afraid of? God told Isaiah not to fall into the fear of these people. If you spend too much time around people who obsess over world events and imagine all the worst scenarios, you will fall into fear with them. Instead, walk away from such conversations before they rattle your spirit.

- Who should you be afraid of? God told Isaiah that if he was going to be afraid of something, it should be God Himself. In this case, fear is a respect and awe of who God is. Since He has all power, there is no need to worry about things of this world. God will take care of them in due time.

Father, the world is full of conspiracy theories and fear of the future, but You alone hold all power. I have no need to fear because You are with me. Help me know when to walk away from conversations that threaten my peace and trust in You.

Confidence

*And this is the confidence that we have in him, that,
if we ask any thing according to his will, he heareth us:
and if we know that he hear us, whatsoever we ask, we
know that we have the petitions that we desired of him.*

1 JOHN 5:14–15

- Do you wish you had more confidence? Do you
have doubts and fears? Are you afraid God will not
answer your prayers? This scripture assures us that
we can approach God's throne with confidence if
we have submitted ourselves to His will.

- Did you ever ask your parents for something when
you were a child, only to have them say no? Did you
think they didn't love you? We all have asked for
things that were not good for us. Our parents loved
us enough to say no in order to protect us from
harm. Our heavenly Father is the same, which is
why He says He will give us what we ask as long as
it's in His will. He isn't trying to keep something
good from us; He is protecting us from potential
harm. Do you trust Him? If we place our trust in
God to do what is for our best, we can submit to
His will in confidence.

- How do we know God's will? Through reading
the Bible and prayer, we can learn about God's

character and purpose in this world. Just like with friends and family, we grow closer by being together and talking. God hears us when we pray, and we can hear God through the moving of the Holy Spirit in our hearts and minds. Communication is a two-way street if we take the time to listen as well.

- What if God says no? If God says no to something we want, then we know that it's not in our best interest. God has something better planned for us, but we have to be willing to wait on His timing and trust Him to give us the best outcome possible. The more time we spend with the Father, the more we will align ourselves with His will so that we will ask rightly and He will grant our petitions.

Father, I come to You with confidence, knowing that You hear me and want my best. You are a loving Father who wants to give good gifts to His children. Help me to know Your will so that I can ask rightly and know my requests will be granted.

Burnout

*And let us not be weary in well doing: for in due season
we shall reap, if we faint not. As we have therefore
opportunity, let us do good unto all men, especially
unto them who are of the household of faith.*

GALATIANS 6:9–10

- Do you ever get tired of trying to do good in a world that doesn't appreciate it? Do you feel like you aren't making a difference, so why bother? It's hard to keep going when we can't see results, but God will give us strength if we will keep moving forward.

- What kind of results are you looking for? Sometimes the problem is that we're looking for immediate results in the natural world, but God works on an eternal scale. He can see what our actions today can yield in the future. Your job may only be planting a seed through kindness. If you let a frazzled mother with small children go ahead of you in line, she may not be able or willing to respond with gratitude; however, she may remember your kindness in days to come and wonder why you were different. Eventually, that could lead her to seek God.

- What kind of reward do you seek? Are you doing good deeds in order to get a pat on the back or a smile of gratitude? Or are you seeking to do the will of the Father regardless of how people respond? We are working for God, not man, so our rewards will come from God. They may not come until we get to heaven, but salvation in itself is enough of a blessing to warrant our working for God out of gratitude alone.

- Our behavior shows the glory of God because we don't do it for worldly applause. Whenever you get an opportunity to do good, do it. It doesn't matter if anyone notices. God sees it, and He will bless it. In due season, all those seeds of kindness and goodness will reap rewards, some now and some in eternity. Either way, just keep your eyes on God and you will never burn out.

Father, sometimes I grow weary of doing good. No one seems to appreciate what I do. Yet, I don't work for other people—I work for You. Help me to keep my eyes on You and be obedient to Your commands. I know I will reap joy in due season.

Spiritual Sticky Notes

But the Comforter, which is the Holy Ghost,
whom the Father will send in my name, he shall
teach you all things, and bring all things to your
remembrance, whatsoever I have said unto you.

JOHN 14:26

- Do you need help remembering things sometimes? Maybe you use sticky notes around your house or office to remind you to do things or keep up with information. As Christians we have something even better than sticky notes: we have the Holy Spirit, who will bring to our remembrance what we need to know just when we need to know it.

- Do you use tutorials or help buttons on electronics? When we have trouble figuring out how to complete a task on a new phone or new software, we can hit the little question mark and search for answers. When we have spiritual questions, we can do almost the same thing. Instead of hitting the question mark, though, we can ask the Holy Spirit to show us what we need to do. God sent Him to teach us all things. Whether we're reading the Bible or praying, the Holy Spirit is our tutor, showing us the way.

- Do you worry that if you try to witness to someone, you'll freeze and not know what to say? The

Holy Spirit will bring out the sticky notes. If you are consistently in God's Word, studying and memorizing, then when you need a particular scripture, the Holy Spirit will bring it to your memory. He will guide you and tell you what to say.

- The key is to be reading what God says in the Bible so that you have the information on file. Then when God calls you to speak to someone, you already have what you need. He is faithful to equip you, sometimes with spiritual sticky notes.

Father, I worry that I won't know what to say when I'm witnessing for You, but You have given me the Holy Spirit, who will help me. As I study the Word, put sticky notes on my heart so that the Holy Spirit can call them to my mind when I need them.

Knowledge Is Power

*Now when they saw the boldness of Peter and
John, and perceived that they were unlearned
and ignorant men, they marvelled; and they took
knowledge of them, that they had been with Jesus.*

ACTS 4:13

- Have you ever heard that knowledge is power?
  People put a high level of importance on getting a
  "good" education, but what makes it good? What
  things must we know in order to say that we have
  a good education? Like many things in this world,
  it's subjective. God has a different take on exactly
  what knowledge is power.

- What do you know? Peter and John were fishermen
  before they met Jesus. They didn't go to school or
  study the Torah. They got up every day and went
  out on a boat to catch fish. Then one day, a man
  named Jesus came along and told them to follow
  Him. So, they did. They followed Him, listened to
  Him, and did what He said. After Jesus died on the
  cross and was buried and resurrected, He went
  back to heaven, but He sent the Holy Spirit to the
  believers and sent them out to be witnesses.

- Is it what you know or who you know? The educated
  religious leaders were amazed when they saw the

disciples, who were uneducated fishermen, boldly witnessing. Peter and John may have not known the Torah, but they knew Jesus backward and forward, and it showed. The only knowledge that has real power is knowing Jesus Christ personally. Human wisdom is of a temporal nature, but godly wisdom is eternal. When you know Jesus as Savior, then you have access to eternity with Him in heaven.

- Peter and John were then able to share their knowledge of Christ with others through witnessing. People could see that they knew Jesus, and they sensed the power of the Holy Spirit at work in their speaking and in their lives. That is when knowledge truly is power.

Father, I want to know You better, because real power rests in the knowledge of Christ. It's not just the mental knowledge but the person knowledge that frees me from the power of sin. Knowing You is more important than knowing facts. Help me use my studying to lead me to a greater knowledge of who You are and in a closer walk with You.

Rest in Him

Except the LORD build the house, they labour in vain that build it: except the LORD keep the city, the watchman waketh but in vain. It is vain for you to rise up early, to sit up late, to eat the bread of sorrows: for so he giveth his beloved sleep.

PSALM 127:1–2

- Do you have a side hustle? Society is filled with people hustling and bustling to get ahead. They are trying to climb a corporate ladder, build a strong retirement, and live a life of ease, but most people just seem tired. They work late hours and weekends until they can't even enjoy their daily lives. They miss meaningful moments in an effort to gain something that isn't guaranteed.

- Who is in control of the future? If God doesn't build the house or the retirement portfolio, then it is built in vain. If God isn't Lord over your life, then watching and worrying will be in vain. When we hand everything over to God, then we can know our efforts will not be wasted. The end results may not be what we wanted, but they will be sufficient.

- Is it okay to rest? There are two extremes in our world today: lazy people and workaholics. Somewhere in between is a healthy rest.

- While making wise plans is good, so is taking time to rest. God controls the future, so you can give your worries and your plans over to Him. Worrying will gain you nothing except sleepless nights. Trust in the Lord, and then you can lie down to sleep and rest in Him, knowing He will work all things out for your good.

Father, I grow weary of trying to hustle all day and night. I need the rest that only You can give. Help me to take each day as it comes, trusting You to handle the outcome. Help me to leave my plans and my worries at Your feet so that I can lay my head down in peaceful sleep and rest in You.

The Seasons of Life

*To every thing there is a season, and a time
to every purpose under the heaven.*

ECCLESIASTES 3:1

- Have you ever been through a long winter, a drought, or a rainy spell? It can feel like forever as we wait for the circumstances to change. One drop of rain in a drought or a bit of sunlight between the rain showers can be cause for joy. Nature is full of cycles, and so is our spiritual journey. There are mountains and valleys as we travel along, but they all have their place, and none of them last forever.

- Are you in a season of trials? Are you in a season of joy? The seasons of life come and go like the waves of the ocean on a beach. Whatever season we are in will end, and another will begin.

- How do you manage the transition from one to the other? We don't get much warning when the seasons change. You wake up one morning, and a cold snap has plummeted temperatures down to freezing. What do you do? You put on your coat and carry on. In times of spiritual trial, we need to carry on as normal, regardless of the season.

- How do you prepare for change? If we have developed a close relationship with the Lord and committed to Bible study and prayer, we can move through each season on an even keel. Walking in God's will is like being in the eye of a hurricane: everything around you is stormy and full of chaos, but your spirit is peaceful as it trusts in God to carry you through.

- Seasons come and go, but they are all set to God's timetable. As you walk the beach and wait to see the next wave, keep your eyes on God and be present where you are. There are joys to be had even in the stormy seasons of life. We just have to trust that God's timing is best and make the most of each season.

Father, I know the seasons come and go for a reason, but please help me to see the beauty in each one. I trust Your timing even though I sometimes struggle and want stormy seasons to pass. The end results will be worth it all, so I strive to make the most of each day I have been given, no matter what season of life it is.

Don't Fail to Commit

Commit thy works unto the LORD,
and thy thoughts shall be established.

PROVERBS 16:3

- Have you ever had someone fail to fulfill a commitment to you? It could be as big as failing to fulfill wedding vows or as little as not keeping an appointment. We feel hurt and angry because we were depending on someone else to keep their word. How many times have we failed in our commitments to God? Yet He gives us second chances over and over again. So, how can we do better at keeping our commitments to the Lord?

- What are some ways we fail to commit? There are at least three ways. One, we commit superficially. We say we are committing something to God, but we are actually only doing it for our own interests. It just sounds better to say we are doing it for the Lord. Second, we give God temporary control but then take it back. This is a matter of trust. We want to be in control because we don't trust God to work it for our good. Third, we commit a work to the Lord but fail to do our part. We expect a miracle to fall down while we watch, but God wants us to be involved in His work.

- So, how do you commit your works to the Lord? You pray about what God wants you to do and then do what He tells you to do, leaving the results in His hands. It's a delicate balance between trusting God as if everything depended on Him and working as if everything depended on you.

- The end result of committing our work to the Lord is that our thoughts will be firmly established and not full of worry and anxiety. The burden of the future is not ours to bear, since we cannot control the outcome. We can rest knowing that we have done our part, and the results belong to God. So, commit your works to God and relax your mind, knowing that you are leaving them in His hands for the best results.

Father, I want my mind to be quiet and stayed on You, so I lift up my whole life to You. I ask that You take control and help me to trust in Your spotless character and power to take care of the rest.

Ray of Hope

*It is of the LORD's mercies that we are not consumed,
because his compassions fail not. They are new
every morning: great is thy faithfulness.*

LAMENTATIONS 3:22–23

- Are you surrounded by the sin and sorrow of this world? Do you ever have days when you feel like a complete failure? You are not alone. We all have days when we feel beaten down by failures and negativity, like we just don't want to try again. Yet there is a ray of hope even in the darkness.

- Jeremiah was known as the weeping prophet because he was tasked with bringing the prophecy of God's judgment on the nation of Israel. Yet, even in the midst of the darkness, God showed him a ray of light. One day the nation would be restored. As Christians we know that not only was the nation of Israel restored, but God also sent the Light of the World, Jesus Christ, to bring hope to a lost and dying world.

- Why do we have hope? God sent Christ as a sacrifice for us so that we could experience a new life in Him and eternity in heaven. It's because of His mercies that we are not consumed by the darkness of sin. God had compassion on us then, and

He has compassion on us now. His mercies are new every morning because He is faithful to His children. Every day is a new chance to begin again.

- When you feel like a total failure, what do you do? You get up tomorrow and try again because it's a new day full of new mercies. Our God is faithful, so we can trust Him to restore us and set us on the right path once again. The darkness has no power over His children; it has no power over you. There is always a ray of hope because Christ came to save the ungodly, and God's mercies are new every morning.

Father, I sometimes fall and feel like my failure is complete, but even in my darkest moments there is a ray of hope. Jesus broke the bands of sin and brought light into the darkness, conquering it for all time. Because of that, Your mercies are new every morning and available to all who will accept them. Thank You for the ray of hope, the light in the darkness, Jesus Christ.

All Is Thine

*Thine, O LORD is the greatness, and the power,
and the glory, and the victory, and the majesty:
for all that is in the heaven and in the earth
is thine; thine is the kingdom, O LORD, and
thou art exalted as head above all.*

1 CHRONICLES 29:11

- Does the constant upheaval in the world leave you unsettled and anxious? Do you feel pressed down with worry and stress? When you feel like there is nothing you can count on, remember that God is constant and unchanging. No matter what is going on in the world, God remains the same.

- What is your focal point? You can find stability when you find focus. When dancers or ice skaters are doing spins, they find one spot to return to after each spin. Keeping their eyes on the focal spot prevents dizziness. Our focal point is God so that when we look to Him, the events of the world can't affect us.

- What do you focus on? The right focus helps us to remember who God is because it gives us the right perspective. This verse gives us a list of the Lord's character traits. All greatness, power, glory, victory, and majesty are His. Everything in heaven and everything on earth belongs to God. He is above all things. We don't have to worry because it's not our place. God has it all under control.

- When we remember who He is, then all the chaos that is spinning around us no longer matters. We have our eyes on our focal spot, and we keep returning to Him every time the world seems to spin out of control. When we remember who He is, we are also drawn to praise Him because everything we have we owe to Him. There is nothing He can't handle, and we can trust Him to fulfill His purposes no matter how chaotic the world becomes. So, get your eyes on your focal point and lift your praises to Him, and the spinning world will cease to distress you as the peace of God settles your soul.

Father, as the world spins around me, I look up to You. I remember who You are. All greatness, power, glory, victory, and majesty belong to You. All the earth and heaven belong to You. I belong to You. I can rest assured that all is well because all is Thine, including me.

Tried-and-True

My brethren, count it all joy when ye fall into divers temptations; knowing this, that the trying of your faith worketh patience. But let patience have her perfect work, that ye may be perfect and entire, wanting nothing.

JAMES 1:2–4

- Do you buy new and trendy items or stick to the tried-and-true? But, how do things become tried-and-true?

- If you've seen many commercials or read many product labels, you will notice that they all mention testing. Companies take a product through rigorous testing to make sure that it will meet the standards they have set. The same applies to our faith. If it's never tested, then how will we know if it will meet God's standard of excellence? If we want to be complete, lacking nothing, then we will have to go through some rigorous testing.

- What does it mean by "divers temptations"? Temptation doesn't mean trying to lure you into sin. In this instance the word can be translated "trial" or "testing." So, like the product testing, our faith is tested to build its strength. Just like in lifting weights or exercising, if we don't push muscles, they will never grow. There is some truth to the "no pain, no gain" concept because discomfort is necessary for change to take effect.

- Why count it joy? Joy doesn't necessarily mean happy, but rather it means that we can have a positive outlook by turning the hardships into lessons learned. We can count it joy when we are tested because we know God is at work. God wants you to be mature and complete so that you can face anything and your faith will hold strong. The struggles and testing are an opportunity for growth so that you can become tried-and-true.

Father, I want to have a strong faith. Help me to see times of trial and struggle as opportunities to grow in patience and faith. Help me to have a positive outlook so that I can joy in the lessons learned and move forward in Your strength. As I go through trials, work in my spirit because I want my faith to be proved tried-and-true.

Abundance

*The thief cometh not, but for to steal, and to kill,
and to destroy: I am come that they might have life,
and that they might have it more abundantly.*

JOHN 10:10

- What is your definition of abundance? Many people think that abundance is about material wealth, but it's more about life overflowing in the spiritual sense. Would you like a more abundant life? It's available for the asking.

- Who is the thief? Satan, our enemy, is the thief. Earlier verses in this chapter talk about Jesus as the Shepherd who watches over His sheep. The thief comes with no good intent. He wants to destroy all that he can through false teachings and all manner of evil. The life lived in sin is one of loss and destruction.

- What is abundant life? Christ came to bring us life so that we may not suffer the consequences of sin. He brings light and joy. He brings an abundant life that is richer than anything the enemy could even dream about.

- Are you living the abundant life? Are you enjoying all the benefits of a life with Christ, free from sin? We have a choice. Once we accept Christ as Lord, we can receive all the many blessings laid out before us, or we leave them sitting on the table unopened. The fruits of the Spirit are ours for the taking.

- Worldly wealth is fleeting and hollow, but God's abundance is eternal and unending. The more money you have, the more money you will want. There is never enough to satisfy your cravings, and you are always worried about losing it. There is no fear in the abundant life. Mercies are new every morning, and the Father owns everything. You only need to ask.

Father, I want to live the abundant life in You. The world's wealth is deceitful and unsatisfying. The more I get of it, the more I want. There is never enough. In You, Lord, I find peace, joy, and love that are worth far more than any treasures on earth. Your mercies are new every morning, and You provide for my needs. I look forward to eternity in heaven with You. In the meantime, help me to keep my eyes on what is important in this life so that I can live a life of true abundance.

Forgive and Forget

*For as the heaven is high above the earth, so great is
his mercy toward them that fear him. As far as the
east is from the west, so far hath he removed our
transgressions from us. Like as a father pitieth his
children, so the LORD pitieth them that fear him.*

PSALM 103:11–13

- Have you ever been told to forgive and forget? It
  sounds good in theory, but we humans are not
  quite capable of the forgetting part. If we do forget it for a while, the enemy will bring it back to
  our memory. Do you struggle remembering your
  own sin, kicking yourself for your failures? You
  don't have to do that anymore. In Christ, once we
  confess and repent, our sins no longer exist.

- How far is it between east and west? When we
  confess our sins, God takes them so far away from
  us that they no longer exist to Him. He not only
  forgives but actually forgets. Have you ever asked
  someone for forgiveness and they agreed, only to
  bring it back up later? As humans we have a hard
  time with forgetting. We are still guilty of allowing
  things we have forgiven in the past to affect our
  future. With God that is not so. He will never bring
  it up again because to Him it no longer exists.

- Who are you to hold on to what God has thrown away? God removed your sin and threw it away. Don't go back into the trash and try and dig it out. Let it go. When the enemy tries to remind you of your past, you remind him of his future. Don't let him keep you from being useful to God's work in this world because you are crying over something that God has long since forgotten about. If you must remember it, do so only as a warning not to repeat it.

- God has pity on His children. He does not want them to live in misery. He has joy waiting for you if you will accept it.

Father, I'm thankful for Your forgiveness and that my sins are removed as far as the east is from the west. Help me to forgive and forget when others sin against me, and help me to forgive myself. I want to live the abundant life in You and be of use for kingdom work.

The End-All

*I am Alpha and Omega, the beginning and the
ending, saith the Lord, which is, and which
was, and which is to come, the Almighty.*

REVELATION 1:8

- Does the enemy seem to be winning? Some days it
  feels like good is losing to evil. All over the news and
  social media are examples of hate and violence. It
  seems like a losing battle. Yet, all good stories have
  conflict, but it is the end that matters.

- Alpha and Omega are the first and last letters of the
  Greek alphabet. God is the first, and He will be the
  last. He is the beginning, and He is the end. He isn't
  done with the world, and He isn't done with you.

- The enemy will try to tell you that you can't win
  because the odds are stacked against you. He tries
  to keep your focus on the temporal so that you can't
  see what's going on at an eternal level. What might
  seem as a failure to you could be something God is
  using as part of a victory. We may lose battles here,
  but Christ has already won the victory.

- God is the end-all of everything. Without Him
  you have nothing that is eternal, nothing that can
  change your life, and nothing that can save you from
  sin. With Him you have all these things and more.

- Throughout time, our enemies have tried to use intimidation and taunting to make us cave without even trying, but talk is cheap. When God spoke in the beginning, the world was created. When He speaks, things happen. When the enemy speaks, it is nothing but a lie. It has no power except what you give it.

- God isn't through either. Revelation is a book about what is to come. You may not understand it all, but in the end God wins, and the end is all you need to know.

Father, the world is a dark place, and sometimes it seems like evil is winning, but I know that You are Alpha and Omega. You have been from the beginning and You know what is to come. The enemy is working harder, and his time is drawing to an end, but You are only just beginning. Help me to have peace even when the enemy is yelling over the battle lines. You are the end-all of everything, and the end is all I need to know.

Who Else?

Who is like unto thee, O LORD, among the gods?
who is like thee, glorious in holiness, fearful in praises,
doing wonders? Thou stretchedst out thy right hand,
the earth swallowed them. Thou in thy mercy hast led
forth the people which thou hast redeemed: thou hast
guided them in thy strength unto thy holy habitation.

EXODUS 15:11–13

- Have you ever heard the phrase "you are something else"? It usually means you're odd in some way and is not necessarily a compliment. God, on the other hand, truly is something else. He can do what no others can. Are you feeling overwhelmed by the enemy? Does it seem like everyone has teamed up against you? Don't worry because God is a God who can.

- These verses are from a song of Moses about God's defeat of Israel's enemies after they fled Egypt. Even though Pharaoh had let them go, he sent the army after them until at one point they were trapped between the Red Sea and the enemy, but God did what only He could do: He parted the Red Sea, and the Israelites crossed on dry land, but as soon as the last Israelite stepped onto shore, God released the waters and swallowed the enemy in the waters.

- Who is like God? There is no one like God, who is glorious in holiness, fearful in praises, and doing wonders like defeating the Egyptian army. He also protected and guided the Israelites. Now they would have a tabernacle for God to inhabit. We don't have to go to the tabernacle to commune with God because He went even further in sending His Son to die on the cross for our sins, making a way for salvation for all mankind.

- When the enemy tries to intimidate you, remind him that God is like no other. Who else is like Him? No one. All else fades in comparison to His glorious holiness. Only He can save. Who else would you turn to?

Father, You parted the Red Sea so that Your children could cross on dry land, and You defeated their enemies without anyone drawing a sword. You guided them across the desert to the promised land. You came and dwelled among Your people in the tabernacle, and now You have made a way for us to join You in heaven. Who else is like You? No one.

Everlasting Love

The Lord hath appeared of old unto me, saying,
Yea, I have loved thee with an everlasting love:
therefore with lovingkindness have I drawn thee.

JEREMIAH 31:3

- Do you have an everlasting love? There are countless songs and movies about it, but is human love truly everlasting? Everything on this earth is temporal and subject to change based on feelings that can turn with the breeze. God's love, on the other hand, is everlasting because He loved us before we were even born and will love us forever. His love will never change.

- Do you feel unlovable? An everlasting love is based not on the object of affection but on the character of the one who loves. God knew us before we were born, and yet He loved us. He knew us when we were living in sin, but He still called us. This love is not dependent on who we are or what we have done. It's based purely on the fact that God is love itself. You only have to accept His gift to you.

- God appeared in ancient days, but He was also with Jeremiah and He is with us. It wasn't just an ancient love; it was an everlasting love, a love for all times. His love was steady even when the children of Israel were disobedient. His love was with them even in captivity. His love will be with us even when we stray from the path of righteousness. God is always faithful to lead His people back to Himself.

- God has drawn us out with loving-kindness away from sin and death and into light and life where we can commune with Him without a mediator. He overlooks our faults and continues to call us to Him. One day we will be with Him face-to-face, but in the meantime we have an everlasting love.

Father, You have loved me with an everlasting love, even when I was trapped in my sin. You drew me with loving-kindness so that I could spend eternity with You. I'm thankful that Your love doesn't depend on who I am or what I have done. I'm thankful You loved me enough to send Your Son to the cross so that I could be forgiven. Eternity is not long enough to praise You for Your everlasting love.

The Plan

According as he hath chosen us in him before
the foundation of the world, that we should
be holy and without blame before him in love.

EPHESIANS 1:4

- Do you make plans? Do they ever fall apart? It's a given that all plans of man are subject to abrupt changes, sometimes on a daily basis. However, the plans of God are written in red, the blood of Christ, and they are unfailing. His plans will come to fruition in His time.

- Do you ever struggle because the plans you made didn't happen the way you thought they should? We can get angry, but God is only looking out for our well-being. He only wants the best for us, so sometimes interrupting our plans is for our benefit.

- Whose plans are they? The other problem is that we tend to make our own plans without asking what God's will is for our lives. We want what we want, and then we are upset when the outcome is not what we had planned. When we accept Jesus Christ as Lord, we accept His lordship over our lives. It's a full surrender. We should be asking God what His will is before we make plans.

- What are His plans? God made a plan before the foundation of the world that we should be adopted children. He made a way for us by sending Christ as a sacrifice so that we could receive forgiveness and eternal life. His plans are always going to be better than our plans because His thoughts are greater than our thoughts.

- So, what are your plans? In the eternal scheme, we are better served to ask God what He wants us to do and leave it to His discretion. When we do plan, we should ask for His will and plan accordingly because His plans never fail.

Father, I often make plans without Your input, and they often fail. I want to join You in Your plan for my life because I know You want the best for me. Help me to know Your will and make plans that follow Your purpose for me today. I thank You for Your eternal plan that made a way for me to be an adopted child and live in eternity with You. It was the best plan of all.

A Large Place

He brought me forth also into a large place;
he delivered me, because he delighted in me.

PSALM 18:19

- Have you ever been surprised by God's gracious-ness? Has God brought you into a large place? When God blesses us beyond our imagination, we have a tendency to either feel like we don't deserve it or become puffed up and think we did something to deserve it. David tells us that God brought him into a large place because of His good will, not because David had done something to deserve it. God gifts His children from His own good will.

- What does God want you to do with your blessings? Don't be like the rich man who just built a bigger barn to store his overflow of grain. Find a way to share it with others, and God will continue to bless it as He gets the glory.

- God delights in His children. Sometimes He gives us daily manna, and sometimes He fills the storehouse. As Paul pointed out, we should learn to be content in whatever situation God puts us and to have an open hand and an open heart. That is something God will always bless.

Father, thank You for Your blessings both great and small. Help me to use what You give me wisely. Show me how to live with open hands and an open heart so that Your blessings can flow through me to others. Help me to remember that all good things come from Your good will and not of my own merit, so that You receive the glory and honor.

Unlimited Supply

*If any of you lack wisdom, let him ask of
God, that giveth to all men liberally, and
upbraideth not; and it shall be given him.*

JAMES 1:5

- When you think of wisdom, do you picture an older
person in a rocking chair doling out advice to the
younger generation? Many people believe wisdom
comes from experience, but the true source of
wisdom is God, and He gives it to all who ask.

- Wisdom is not just for the old. When Solomon
took the throne after King David died, God told
him to ask for anything, and he asked for wisdom.
Solomon was considered one of the wisest men
of his time, even though he was probably only in
his twenties. Wisdom served him well during his
reign as Israel's king.

- Wisdom is not just knowledge; it's knowing how
to apply knowledge to given situations. It begins
with the fear, or respect, of God, which leads to
right living and results in an increased ability to
know right from wrong. Wisdom is knowing when
to be quiet and when to speak up. It's being able to
choose the right path. Wisdom is not a guarantee
that you won't make a mistake because we are all

human, but it will make it easier to make decisions and get back on the right path when you stray.

- How do you get wisdom? First of all, you have to ask for it. Then you have to use it. If you are trying to live in God's will by reading the Word, praying for guidance, and walking in obedience, then God will give it to you. There is not an age requirement, so ask for wisdom daily and God will grant it without fail. You don't have to worry about supply issues because this is a gift God does not put limitations on. He gives it liberally and never fusses when you ask for seconds.

Father, I need wisdom as I live in this fallen world. The enemy is always at work trying to trip me up, but Your wisdom shows me how to live and make the best possible choices. Help me to ask for wisdom every day and use it for Your glory. I'm thankful that You have an unlimited supply that You will give to all who ask, without limitations.

Topical Index

SCRIPTURE INDEX

Looking for More Encouragement for Your Heart?

Worry Less, Pray More

This purposeful devotional guide features 180 readings and prayers designed to help alleviate your worries as you learn to live in the peace of the almighty God, who offers calm for your anxiety-filled soul.

Paperback / 978-1-68322-861-5

Too Blessed to be Stressed: 3-Minute Devotions for Women

You'll find the spiritual pick-me-up you need in *Too Blessed to be Stressed: 3-Minute Devotions for Women*. These 180 uplifting readings from best-selling author Debora M. Coty pack a powerful dose of inspiration, encouragement, humor, and faith into just-right-sized readings for your busy schedule.

Paperback / 978-1-63409-569-3